Combatting Corruption in the Commonwealth Caribbean

Edited by Roger Koranteng

Commonwealth Secretariat
Marlborough House
Pall Mall
London SW1Y 5HX
United Kingdom

https://thecommonwealth.org/

Published by the Commonwealth Secretariat

Views and opinions expressed in this publication are the responsibility of the authors and should in no way be attributed to the institutions to which they affiliated or to the Commonwealth Secretariat.

Wherever possible, the Commonwealth Secretariat uses paper sourced from responsible forests or from sources that minimise a destructive impact on the environment.

A catalogue record for this publication is available from the British Library.

ISBN (print): 978-1-84859-997-0
ISBN (e-book): 978-1-84859-985-7

Printed and bound by CPI Group (UK) Ltd, Croydon, CR0 4YY

Contents

Foreword

Improving integrity by strengthening systems, procedures and regulatory provision is a longstanding Commonwealth priority. It is through such positive approaches that we tackle the negative and destructive impact of corruption on the lives, livelihoods and well-being of people in all our member countries. The resources amounting to billions if not trillions of dollars which are misappropriated by the corrupt practices of the greedy and pernicious few are the very funds we need in order to answer in practical ways the hopes and aspirations contained in our Commonwealth Charter 2013 and to deliver on the commitments adopted by our members in 2015 through the Sustainable Development Goals.

This publication draws together examples of action taken by six Commonwealth countries in the Caribbean to deal with corruption, examining what works and also sharing lessons of interventions that have proved quite effective as well as the challenges which need continued attention. Our aim is for our member countries to build together in a spirit of goodwill and mutual support, putting the 'common' into 'wealth', and 'wealth' into 'Commonwealth', for the greater good and progress of all communities and people.

The Rt Hon Patricia Scotland QC

The Secretary-General of the Commonwealth

Preface

Across the Commonwealth, work to help fight corruption is delivered by the Secretariat through strategies of establishing regional anti-corruption agency networks and training centres to facilitate closer cooperation and learning. For example, the Commonwealth Caribbean Association of Integrity Commissions and Anti-Corruption Bodies, created by the Commonwealth Secretariat, has promoted collaboration and the exchange both of best practice and of practitioners among member countries in the region.

Commonwealth Anti-Corruption Benchmarks have also been designed to further help governments and public sector bodies. They allow for anti-corruption laws, procedures and actions to be measured against international good practice. The 22 Benchmarks cover topics from sanctions for corruption offences to investigating and prosecuting authorities, and from political lobbying to disclosure of asset ownership.

This book, *Combatting Corruption in the Commonwealth Caribbean*, has been prepared by the Public Sector Governance Unit of the Commonwealth Secretariat to highlight the ways in which six Commonwealth Caribbean countries have made significant progress in combatting the problem: The Bahamas, Barbados, Dominica, Grenada, St Lucia and St Vincent and the Grenadines. These countries have been selected due to their relatively strong scores on Transparency International's Corruption Perceptions Index (CPI) or because they have registered a significant improvement in their score on this index over the past decade.

The CPI ranks countries by their perceived levels of public sector corruption according to experts and businesspeople. It measures certain aspects of public sector corruption, including bribery, use of public office for private gain, nepotism in the public service, state capture, government's ability to enforce integrity mechanisms, legal protection for whistle-blowers, journalists and investigators, the existence of adequate laws on financial disclosure, conflict of interest prevention and access to information.

The book identifies the factors and institutions within these six countries that have contributed to the reduction of the impact of corruption and tries to account for the elements – both technical and political – that have enabled them to implement successful anti-corruption strategies. It includes lessons learnt, challenges and recommendations.

This book, which researches into the 'islands of success' in the fight against corruption, is aimed primarily at key stakeholders in the Commonwealth Caribbean. The overall aim of the project is to produce a resource that will help governments and other stakeholders to learn from the experiences of countries that have been successful in reducing corruption and encourage them to review their current practice and to ensure the promotion of good governance.

Acknowledgements

Special thanks go to the six researchers who were commissioned to undertake the countries studies under the overall direction and supervision of Head, Public Sector Governance Unit, Governance and Peace Directorate, Commonwealth Secretariat, Dr Roger Koranteng. They are Lemarque A Campbell who was responsible for The Bahamas study, Dirk Harrison who did the Barbados study, Julian Johnson conducted the Dominica study, Colin McDonald for the Grenada study, Dawn De Coteau and EMA Solutions Management Consultancy who led the St Lucia study, and Matthew Goldie-Scott of Thuso Ltd who undertook the St Vincent and the Grenadines study.

We would like to thank the Integrity Commissions in St Lucia, Grenada and Dominica, the Office of the Attorney-Generals in Barbados, St Vincent and the Grenadines and Bahamas for the immense assistance towards the study. Finally, we would like to express our gratitude to all those individuals and institutions across private, public, and civil society who made invaluable contributions to the study.

Acronyms and abbreviations

ACAMS	Association of Certified Money Laundering Specialists
AML	Anti-Money Laundering
CARICOM	Caribbean Community
CBI	Citizen By Investment
CCAICACB	Commonwealth Caribbean Association of Integrity Commissions and Anti-Corruption Bodies
CDB	Caribbean Development Bank
CFATF	Caribbean Financial Action Task Force
CFT	Combating the Financing of Terrorism
CPI	Corruption Perception Index
CSO	civil society organisation
DPP	Director of Public Prosecutions
EU	European Union
FATF	Financial Action Task Force
FIA	Financial Intelligence Authority
FOIA	Freedom of Information Act, The Bahamas
FRA	Fiscal Responsibility Act, Grenada
FROC	Fiscal Responsibility Oversight Committee, Grenada
FSRA	Financial Services Regulatory Authority, St Lucia
FSSU	Financial Sector Supervision Unit, St. Lucia
FTRA	Financial Transactions Reporting Act, The Bahamas
GARFIN	Grenada Authority for the Regulation of Financial Institutions
GDP	gross domestic product
GIC	Grenada Integrity Commission
IACAC	Inter American Convention Against Corruption
ICRG	International Co-Operation Review Group

IDB	Inter-American Development Bank
IMF	International Monetary Fund
MESICIC	Follow-Up Mechanism for the Implementation of the IACAC
MLPA	Money Laundering Prevention Act
MP	Member of Parliament
OAG	Office of the Attorney General
OAS	Organization of American States
ODPP	Office of the Director of Public Prosecutions
OECD	Organisation for Economic Co-operation and Development
OECS	Organisation of Eastern Caribbean States
ORG	Organization for Responsible Government, The Bahamas
POCA	Proceeds of Crime Act
RBOA	Register of Beneficial Ownership Act, The Bahamas
RBPF	Royal Barbados Police Force
SLDB	St Lucia Development Bank
STR	Serious Transaction Reports
SVG	St Vincent and the Grenadines
SVGHRA	SVG Human Rights Association
UNCAC	United Nations Convention against Corruption
UNODC	United Nations Office on Drugs and Crime
WGI	World Governance Indicators

Chapter 1

Introduction

Roger Koranteng

This book focuses on six Commonwealth Caribbean countries that have made significant progress in combating the problem of corruption. Each of these countries – The Bahamas, Barbados, Dominica, Grenada, St Lucia and St Vincent and the Grenadines – is considered in a separate chapter that examines the specific factors and institutions that have contributed to the reduction of the impact of corruption and tries to account for the elements, both technical and political, that have enabled it to implement successful anti-corruption strategies.

The six countries have been selected due to their relatively strong scores on Transparency International's Corruption Perceptions Index (CPI) or because they have registered a significant improvement in their score on this index over the past decade. The CPI ranks countries by their perceived levels of public sector corruption according to experts and businesspeople. The aspects of corruption considered include bribery, use of public office for private gain, nepotism in the public service, state capture, government's ability to enforce integrity mechanisms, legal protection for whistle-blowers, journalists and investigators, the existence of adequate laws on financial disclosure, conflict of interest prevention and access to information.

All the countries discussed here have signed the Inter-American Convention Against Corruption (IACAC), a regional convention that promotes and strengthens the development by each of the States Parties of the mechanisms needed to prevent, detect, punish and eradicate corruption. The Bahamas, Dominica, Grenada and St Lucia are also parties to the United Nations Convention Against Corruption (UNCAC), the first global multilateral anti-corruption instrument, while Barbados has signed the convention but not ratified it. The UNCAC covers different forms of corruption, such as bribery, abuse of functions and trading in influence, and it provides for prevention measures, criminalization and law enforcement, international cooperation, asset recovery, technical assistance, and information exchange.

The studies provides novel research and analysis on each country's anti-corruption initiatives, particularly on: the legal and institutional frameworks aimed at mitigating corruption in the country; how groups such as the private sector, the media, civil society and international and regional organisations have contributed to anti-corruption efforts; some of the challenges that the country faces in its anti-corruption efforts; and how lessons could be applied elsewhere in the Commonwealth Caribbean.

The Bahamas: Over the past five years, The Bahamas has remained among the top 30 least corrupt countries in the world as measured by the CPI. Its economy is heavily reliant on tourism and financial services, and the latter was significantly impacted a few years ago as international bodies considered the jurisdiction to be a tax haven and conduit for money laundering. Since 2017, however, the Government has made significant steps to enhance its anti-money laundering regime and implement all the necessary reforms to address international concerns regarding economic substance, preferential exemptions for foreign entities and lack of automatic exchange of tax information with other jurisdictions.

There is no single anti-corruption agency in The Bahamas. Instead, its anti-corruption framework spans a compendium of laws and government institutions that work in tandem to reduce corruption in the country. These efforts are led by the Office of the Prime Minister, setting the 'tone at the top'. Currently, there are over 13 pieces of legislation that have been brought into force, covering a range of offences, along with over 11 institutions that provide the backing for the anti-corruption framework. For example, the *Proceeds of Crime Act, 2018* introduced Unexplained Wealth Orders, which provide the Director of Public Prosecutions with a mechanism to apply to the Court to enquire into the finances of an individual charged with an offence such as bribery, money laundering or misconduct in public office. And the *Freedom of Information Act, 2017*, has a provision regarding whistleblowing, which is regarded as a highly effective anti-corruption and democratic accountability mechanism that may lead to widespread reforms, enhancing the quality of life for society at large.

The judiciary in The Bahamas was regarded as the least corrupt public institution, among all assessed government institutions, in the 2020 World Justice Project Rule of Law Index.

Since 2017, the Identified Risk Framework Steering Committee has been meeting at least once per week to focus on common issues, emerging risks and risk containment by examining procedures, policies, legislation, guidelines and government structures. As a result of the Committee's hard work, The Bahamas was successfully removed from the Financial Action Task Force's (FATF) grey list in 2020. Countries on the FATF grey list represent a much higher risk of money laundering and terrorism financing.

In recent years, the Government has made a concerted effort to consult with industry leaders and private sector organisations on draft legislation that relates to anti-corruption reforms. Consultations are usually held before the draft legislation is tabled in Parliament for debate. The Government has also invited numerous private sector bodies to participate and present during the UNCAC and IACAC country review processes. In addition, it has developed a number of consultative channels with leading civil society organisations (CSOs). Press freedom is constitutionally guaranteed and generally respected in practice, and the media play an active role in exposing corruption matters.

The Government collaborates with regional and international partners on initiatives to assist in its anti-corruption efforts. For example, The Bahamas is part of the Commonwealth Caribbean Association of Integrity Commissions and Anti-Corruption Bodies (CCAICACB), an initiative established by the Commonwealth Secretariat to bring all anti-corruption professional bodies in the region together to organise common, focused, and targeted assistance to member countries. In addition, it participates in the Follow-Up Mechanism for the Implementation of the IACAC (MESICIC), which is the Anti-Corruption Mechanism of the Organization of American States (OAS). The OAS also provides The Bahamas with anti-corruption technical assistance.

Despite these various initiatives, The Bahamas still faces a number of challenges in its anti-corruption framework and efforts. These include a lack of regulations on the financing of political parties and candidates running for elected office; the lack of a law or clear policy to address the 'revolving door' (the movement of individuals between public office and private sector while working on the same sector issue); the failure of some parliamentarians to disclose their assets, income and liabilities with no criminal action taken; and the lack of trustworthy independent reporting channels to support whistle-blowers.

Barbados: Over the past 10 years, Barbados has consistently ranked on the CPI as the least corrupt country in the region. It is arguable that this is due to its stable economy, low crime rate enhanced by law enforcement and independent judicial system.

Barbados has an open market economy, with services, manufacturing and agriculture being the most significant sectors. It receives high remittances from Barbadians overseas and has a relatively high per capita income. Tourism is vital to the economy as the chief foreign exchange earner as well as a major employer.

There exists a primary legal and institutional framework in the country for combatting corruption, and there is a culture of discipline and maintenance of the rule of law. Barbadians have a strong sense of nationalism and high levels of social order, and the roles of the police and the education system have in a significant way defined the attributes of self-discipline, honesty and orderliness. Most youth and adults are committed to respecting law enforcement authorities and more so the rule of law, presumably strongly settled in the belief system that good behaviour is rewarded, and bad behaviour is not.

The Government has made it a priority to strengthen the anti-corruption framework through its legal structure and a whole-of-community approach. Most recently, the *Anti-Corruption and Anti-Terrorism Agency Act (2021)* was passed by the Senate in 2021. There have also been important amendments to existing laws to include the *Money Laundering and Financing of Terrorism (Amendment) (Prevention and Control) Act, 2019, Money Laundering and Financing of Terrorism (Prevention and Control) (Amendment) (No.2) Act, 2019* and *Anti-Terrorism (Amendment) Act, 2019.* In addition, the Government has indicated its intention to strengthen the anti-corruption framework by the passage of the Freedom of Information Bill and the Whistle-blowers Protection Bill.

The Government has had several engagements with the private and civil sectors, the media and international organizations. For example, the Integrity Group Barbados (a local CSO), the Bar Association and other stakeholders have been invited within the last three years to engage with the Government through submissions on critical pieces of legislation concerning the anti-corruption regime. The Integrity Group Barbados has also participated in roundtable discussions, International Anti-Corruption Day celebrations and advocacy related to the anti-corruption agenda. During 2014 to 2016, the Inter-American Development Bank (IDB 2017) funded the modernization of the Barbados National Procurement System, and the United Nations Office on Drugs and Crime (UNODC) conducted workshops towards implementation and ratification of the UNCAC and facilitated training in anti-corruption strategies in conjunction with the Office of the Attorney General.

Some continuing challenges include the lack of institutional capacity in the Police Service to tackle corruption, with its Financial Crime Investigation Unit – created to probe public corruption, fraud and terrorism financing – lacks expertise and human resources. There are also no campaign financing laws or modern regulations governing spending by candidates during an election campaign. Moreover, the Barbados parliamentary caucus has encountered issues with the timely passing of several important Bills. The Government is also experiencing a data deficit gap, with improvement needed in the collection and storage of data and in making them available to be utilised as a measuring tool to assess the anti-corruption framework.

Dominica: Dominica has a long tradition of integrity and professionalism in its public service, due mainly to a supportive legal framework and careful selection and training of its public servants. Very few incidents of corruption have occurred over the past 60 years. The Government has also strengthened provisions for accountability and transparency in its legislation and institutions for audit, finance administration and the prevention of money laundering. It has recently enacted legislation for public procurement and contract administration and for integrity in public office. Significantly, the latter brought within its ambit a classification of 'persons in public life', which includes the Cabinet, MPs and non-elected public officials who were not previously directly covered by the regulatory statutes.

Reform measures were also taken to establish and strengthen oversight institutions, including a new Central Procurement Board to ensure transparency and fairness in procurement contracts for goods, services and works; a financial services unit to oversee the operations of financial institutions; and an Integrity Commission to, inter alia, inquire into allegations of bribery and acts of corruption. As regards the operations of central Government, major reforms were carried out to systems and procedures to strengthen real-time integrated accounting and auditing to streamline and secure government financial transactions and produce timely and accurate reports and for real-time internal audit purposes.

The major institutions engaged in corruption prevention have reached out to the public to gain their support in carrying out their functions as oversight and enforcement bodies. Recent experience has shown that legislation and institutional frameworks must be regularly reviewed and strengthened to allow for enhanced autonomy for and parliamentary oversight of oversight bodies. In addition, there should be vigorous public education and engagement on the deleterious effects of corruption in societies.

The vigour of government support for and the consistency of its commitment to the fight against corruption is critical for any measure of success to be achieved. All three political parties have committed to taking strong action to combat corruption. There is, therefore, consensus in Parliament as to the objective of safeguarding the society from the corrosive and debilitating effects of corruption. The Government continues to provide all the oversight bodies with adequate budgets to finance their operations; the budgets of the Integrity Commission, the Director of Audit and the DPP, in keeping with their status as independent bodies, are provided by law.

The Integrity Commission has also kept up with its mandate to receive declarations on the financial affairs of persons in public life and to investigate and report on any breach of its Code of Conduct or other acts of corruption. It is a founding member of the CCAICACB. Through its outreach programmes to gain public understanding and support, the Commission has also initiated effective measures to engage with public officials and the public.

The print media in Dominica continues to play an important role, is relatively free and independent and boldly highlights issues surrounding mismanagement of public affairs. The role of social media has also gained traction in recent years.

The country continues to face some challenges. As a trans-shipment point for narcotics, it is affected by the international narcotics market, and the laundering of money made outside the country is a major issue. The presence of an unknown number of offshore financial institutions with no published beneficial ownership heightens the risk. The work of the Integrity Commission is restricted by the legal requirement to act only on complaints received and not on its own volition. It also requires high level management and professional staff who are suitably qualified and have the necessary experience and capacity to perform its high statutory purpose of advancing probity, integrity and accountability among high-level state functionaries. Moreover, public support for oversight bodies in general, and the Integrity Commission in particular, is a crucial issue. Public awareness and understanding of the role and purpose of these institutions is at best superficial, and this is exacerbated by the deep divide between political communities and strong adherence to party loyalties. Related to the latter point, laws are lacking on the way political parties and election campaigns are financed.

Grenada: Grenada's scores on the CPI over the last five years have been well above the average. This is particularly noteworthy as, during the late 1990s and early part of the 2000s, the country was seen as a haven for fraudulent off-shore banking transactions and suffered much reputational damage. However, the Government then moved decisively to strengthen institutional arrangements to address corruption and promote good governance. It was aware that a whole-of-government approach to combatting corruption was needed, including the enactment of legislation, the establishment of new organizations and the acceptance of regional and international standards.

Among the new legislation, the Integrity in Public Life Act No. 24. of 2013 set up the Grenada Integrity Commission (GIC), an amendment to which in 2015 provides for the GIC to receive and verify the accuracy of declarations of financial affairs from public officials; to investigate complaints of impropriety, corruption and misconduct by public officials; and for prosecution of persons found guilty of crimes. The GIC has also set up the Integrity Commission Round Table through which it works with stakeholders to monitor, uncover and mitigate all aspects/reports of corruption in public bodies. In addition, it has a strong public education and advocacy programme with a special focus on young people, recognising that change begins with education. It has received on-site training by world experts from commonwealth Secretariat and the UNODC in international best practices.

A Financial Intelligence Unit (FIU) was also set up to prevent, detect, investigate and control financial crimes. Sharing of information between the GIC and the FIU is a necessary condition for inter-agency co-operation in combating corruption and financial crime and enables the agencies to work together to their mutual benefit. In addition to sharing information, it enables an investigation team to draw on a wider range of skills and experience from investigators with different backgrounds and training. The net effect of these measures and strategies is the creation of an environment that is less likely to facilitate corrupt behaviour by public officers. There is also a Grenada Authority for the Regulation of Financial Institutions (GARFIN), which regulates the entire non-bank financial sector, thereby consolidating supervision for the administration of 12 pieces of legislation. GARFIN has implemented a system of off-site and on-site supervision and conducted its first inspection of money services.

In an effort to address the reputational damage that the island suffered during the banking fiasco, Grenada opened itself to global scrutiny so as to align its institutions and laws to that of acceptable regional and international standards. Mainly through the GIC, it has forged alliances, signed on to international conventions and treaties and participated in regional and international forums as it attempts to address corruption and promote good governance. In January 2002, the country reaffirmed its commitment to the inter-American system by ratifying a series of Organization of American States (OAS) conventions on the fight against corruption, terrorism and arms trafficking. It has also become a member of the CCAICACB. By way of all these initiatives Grenada has built organisational structures, strengthened its human resource capabilities, built international networks and inserted itself into the international and regional frameworks aimed at fighting corruption.

The smallness of society in islands such as Grenada means individuals constantly interact. This creates an environment where reporting acts of corruption may be challenging because of the possibility of being targeted and labelled as an informer. This situation serves to reinforce the reluctance to be a whistle-blower and as such has left room for corruption to grow, even in the face of improvements in legislation and oversight institutions. However, Grenada demonstrates that, with strong political will, a country with a high level of corruption can be transformed to a low corruption country. Anti-corruption agencies and key stakeholder organisations work collaboratively to promote learnings that can then lead to improvements in systems and processes. The island's media also plays a very active role in the fight against corruption by way of advocacy and sensitisation.

St Lucia: St Lucia has ranked above the world average and scored as one of the top four countries in the Caribbean region in the CPI for over 10 years. This consistently high score has demonstrated that the country continues to make great strides in progressing the anti-corruption agenda across legal and institutional frameworks. Moreover, St Lucia has been recognised for its significant progress in addressing and improving its anti-money laundering and combating the finance of terrorism regime and is no longer subject to rigorous Caribbean Financial Action Task Force or International Co-Operation Review Group monitoring.

St Lucia has enacted/established a raft of legal and primary institutional frameworks to assist in combating corruption. For example, the *Integrity in Public Life Act* covers financial disclosure for persons in public life, declaration of receipts of gifts and specific corruption acts; the *Audit Act No.26 of 1988* provides for the Director of Audit to scrutinise the accounts relating to consolidated funds, public bodies, statutory bodies and government companies; and *The Procurement and Asset Disposal Act (2015)* strengthens the procurement procedures in key respects, providing guarantees that tendering processes are open. It also provides mechanisms to ensure that the government agents who procure do not have conflicts of interest.

St Lucia has several institutions that are assisting in the anti-corruption agenda. As well as operating as regulatory institutions, these organisations also undertake stakeholder engagement. The main anti-corruption body is the Integrity Commission, whose key function is to obtain written declarations of the assets, liabilities and income of Senators and Members of Parliament (MPs). In addition, it has engaged in country-wide public education and awareness-building programmes focusing on the importance of 'integrity' and removing the emphasis purely on 'corruption'. The Financial Intelligence Authority (FIA) has the mandate of detecting, preventing and prosecuting money laundering and other serious crimes as well as confiscating the proceeds of crime, while the Office of the Director of Audit was set up to promote greater accountability in the public service through monitoring and reporting on the efficiency, economy and effectiveness of government spending. These anti-corruption agencies all operate independent of government, which ensures they are able to function without government interference and further allows them to undertake their roles objectively.

The CSO sector is not as developed in St Lucia as other larger Caribbean countries and there is none that focuses on anti-corruption. In terms of involvement with regional and international organisations, St Lucia is a member of the CCAICACB. In addition, the Saint Lucia Crime Victimization Survey was conducted by UNODC, making it the first Caribbean country to measure victimisation in line with international United Nations standards. The data and wider learning from the survey emphasise the importance of implementing preventative measures against crime.

There is no doubt that St Lucia has made positive strides to ensure that corruption is addressed. It has enacted preventative measures such as asset declaration provisions and codes of ethical conduct to ensure that persons in public life are operating with integrity. However, in order to provide appropriate sanctions, agencies such as the Integrity Commission depend on citizens to report acts of corruption and such reporting appears to be very low. In continuing with its progress in building a robust anti-corruption regime, the Government should consider ways in which it is engaging with the various stakeholders to prevent corrupt practices occurring.

These could include a clear policy mandate, systems to detect acts of corruption – i.e., financial disclosure systems for government and public officials – and public education programmes. There is also a lack of anti-corruption data, with none of the public agencies posting relevant statistics online. Of note, there was no dedicated Integrity Commission website.

St Vincent and the Grenadines: St Vincent and the Grenadines (SVF) is one of the highest scoring countries in the region, ranking seventh on the CPI, as well as being the fourth highest Commonwealth member state in the Caribbean and Americas, with only Canada, the Bahamas and Barbados achieving higher scores. It appears to have a satisfactory rule of law and widespread confidence in the capabilities of law enforcement agencies, which increases the likelihood of wrongdoers being reported and improves trust in the law. Additionally, the country has legislative frameworks that address anti money laundering, and it has been collaborating closely with the U.S. Department of State as well as other Commonwealth countries on anti-corruption initiatives and related criminal matters. The country continues to undertake reforms, and there appear to be good opportunities for bipartisan support for improved transparency and anti-corruption measures moving forward, thereby facilitating economic development and improved investor confidence.

A number of key laws has been identified as contributing to the fight against corruption in the country. These include the *Prevention of Corruption Act, 2004,* which is intended to prevent corruption in the performance of public functions and give effect to the provisions of the ICAC; the *Financial Intelligence Unit Act, 2001* (amended in 2009), which establishes a Financial Intelligence Unit (FIU) to be 'the national centralised unit … for the collection, analysis and dissemination of suspicious transaction information to competent authorities'; and the *Public Procurement Act, 2018,* among others.

The main oversight bodies are the Office of the Attorney General, the Office of the Director of Public Prosecutions, the Audit Department and the Service Commissions Department of the Public Service Commissions. The Audit Department was established to examine government accounts to ensure that funds provided by Parliament are used for the purposes intended. It works with the Public Accounts Committee, which is appointed by the House of Assembly to, inter alia, report any excess or unauthorised expenditure of public funds the reasons for such expenditure.

In general, there is broad consensus that the judiciary generally operates independently. Complaints against the police are submitted by the public through the Public Relations and Complaints Department, or any police station, and are reported to be addressed effectively, though a lack of publicly available statistics on the number of prosecutions and convictions of police officers for misconduct or corruption has the potential to undermine the transparency of the process.

CSOs active in anti-corruption in the country include the SVG Human Rights Association (SVGHRA), which promotes and encourages respect for human rights and fundamental freedoms through education, training, representation, documentation and advocacy. Likewise, organisations such as Marion House (a social services agency) have contributed actively to policy dialogue and provided concrete recommendations on how transparency and anti-corruption initiatives could be strengthened. The National Council of Women has also made sustained and active contributions, particularly in relation to interactions with the OAS on anti-corruption matters (OAS, 2014b). The SVGHRA has called for a mechanism for monitoring police conduct that has greater transparency than the current system.

Local and regional journalists have been proactive contributors to policy dialogue pertaining to corruption and transparency in SVG. Yet, while freedoms of peaceful assembly and association are protected in law, concerns have been raised by some media and CSOs about fear of retaliation. In such a context, it is essential that both perceived, and actual, freedom of press be prioritised to ensure that the media can continue to play a key role in facilitating transparency and constructive dialogue on policy reforms. The private sector has also engaged proactively in dialogue relating to anti-corruption and transparency initiatives, including substantive consultations during the development of the SVG report on implementing the IACAC. Continued engagement with the private sector is essential if reforms are to be implemented effectively, particularly given the growing significance of the sector to national economic development.

Despite the progress made, challenges remain. For example, although legislative drafting sets out a clear agenda to establish an Integrity Commission as early as 2004, as of 2021, there is no Commission in place, and the necessary legislation to facilitate its establishment has yet to be introduced. Furthermore, freedom of information legislation, passed in 2003, has yet to be introduced and there is no legislation requiring government officials to disclose assets, income or gifts. In addition, SVG is yet to sign the UNCAC.

Challenges

The size, geographic location and stage of development of Small Island Developing States (SIDS), such as those in the Caribbean, mean that these countries literally cannot afford to tolerate acts of corruption. In small islands, decisions in the economic, political and legal fields have a pervasiveness that they lack in large societies. Benedict (1967) contends that this is because people are connected to each other in many different ways in small societies; and in such societies one cannot progress very far occupationally or professionally without coming into contact with the government. Many roles are played by a few individuals, so the same individuals constantly interact.

This has profound implications for economic and social development since decisions and choices of individuals will be influenced by their relations in many contexts with other individuals. This reality creates an environment where reporting acts of corruption may be challenging because of the possibility of being targeted and labelled as an informer. This situation serves to reinforce the reluctance to be a whistle-blower and as such has left room for corruption to grow in the Caribbean, even in the face of improvements in legislation and oversight institutions.

Lessons

The key lessons that can be drawn from the case studies include the following:

- There need to be a robust legislative and institutional anti-corruption framework, with the country's anti-money laundering regime brought to an acceptable international standard. Article 5 of UNCAC requires State parties to periodically evaluate relevant legal instruments and administrative measures with a view to determining their adequacy to prevent and fight corruption.

- There should be an all-of-government approach to combatting corruption and money laundering, with agencies collaborating in collective action initiatives to mitigate corruption risks.

- Improvements in the legislative framework and enhancements to administrative procedures are not sufficient to sustain anti-corruption policies. Constant parliamentary oversight bolstered by the operations of well-ordered and coordinated oversight bodies is the most effective bulwark against corruption in all its forms.

- A fundamental pillar for an efficient and effective anti-corruption body is the possession of high-level professional staff who are loyal to it and its mandate.

- Technical expertise among public officials is also important for an effective and efficient procurement system. Access to information should be a number one rule in procurement procedures.

- Anti-corruption agencies and key stakeholder organisations working collaboratively has the potential to promote learnings that can then lead to improvements in the systems and processes that are used in the fight against corruption.

- Governments should maintain strong engagement with civil society, the private sector and international and regional partners to develop an inclusive approach to its anti-corruption efforts.

- Governments should increase the level of transparency in the management of public finances. With strong political will, a country with a high level of corruption can be transformed to a low corruption country.

- Countries within the Commonwealth must make it a priority to instil values of discipline, law and order from a tender age. These values should be inculcated through the school system, religious institutions, and the family structure.

- Regional and international collaboration has the potential to strengthen domestic anti-corruption initiatives and improve outcomes.

Recommendations

The following recommendations are based on the case studies:

- Governments should seek to incorporate anti-corruption reforms into larger reforms for national development, such as enhancing the ease of doing business or increasing government efficiency, as this will ensure greater support from the citizenry.

- Anti-corruption initiatives should be championed by a senior government official, such as the Prime Minister, to ensure that there is greater buy-in among government agencies.

- There should be an independent and impartial Integrity Commission, allowing international agencies and donors to interface directly and facilitating regular and periodic technical support and training in keeping with emerging and existing international best practices.

- Integrity Commissions and Anti-Corruption Bodies should be staffed by persons who are suitably qualified and possessed the necessary experience and capacity to perform the high statutory purpose of advancing probity, integrity and accountability over powerful and high-level state functionaries.

- Governments should enact effective political campaign finance legislation to ensure that political parties frequently report their finances, including all donations received and expenditures, to an independent election authority. Additionally, they should establish a cap on political campaign spending to limit the influence that money has during elections.

- All relevant government agencies should collaborate on anti-corruption initiatives in a collective action approach. They should also engage with the private sector, civil society and international and regional partners in their anti-corruption efforts, as this will increase both the credibility of these efforts and trust in the government.

- To address the 'revolving door' challenge, governments should ensure that a 'cooling off' period is implemented and enforced in which there is a specified period before senior government officials are allowed to move into private sector entities of which they had oversight.

- Governments should ensure that the judiciary and prosecution remain independent and free from political influence.

- The media and civil society should be guaranteed freedom of expression in practice.

- Effective and innovative anti-corruption public education programmes should be conceptualised and implemented.

- Governments must urgently fast track closing the data deficit gap and prioritise the collection, storage and availability of data that could be utilised and included as a part of a measuring tool to assess the anti-corruption framework.

- The internal regulatory mechanisms of government – accounting and audit, procurement, and personnel – should be the centrepiece of reforms to promote accountability and good governance.

- There should be stricter enforcement of anti-corruption legislation.

- There should be harmonising of the procurement processes at the OECS level, along with transparent cross-regional procurement, particularly of expensive and high-value items. This is particularly so with goods and services that require a service contract over time and where significant value can be sought with a collective approach.

- A whistleblowing hotline should be introduced for persons to report anonymously.

- The use of the newly published Commonwealth Anti-Corruption Benchmarks should be considered to ensure good practice in relation to infrastructure, particularly regarding construction permits and registering property.

- it is recommended that the Benchmarks be utilised to undertake an in-depth review of legislative and procedural frameworks to ensure alignment with international good practice.

Conclusions

It can be argued that the small and close-knit societies such as Caribbean states means they are prone to corruption and other governance issues. However, this study has identified the factors and institutions within the six countries that have contributed to the reduction of the impact of corruption and seeks to account for the factors – both technical and political – that have enabled them to implement successful anti-corruption strategies. The lessons learnt, challenges and recommendations will assist the wider Caribbean states in making further progress in addressing the ongoing challenges of corruption.

Bibliography

AMLA (Anti-Money Laundering Authority) (2019) *Annual Reports 2013–2018.* Bridgetown: Financial Intelligence Unit. https://barbadosfiu.gov.bb/wp-content/uploads/2019/12/FIU-Annual-Report-2013-2018.pdf

Benedict, B (ed.) (1967) *Problems of Smaller Territories. London: Athlone Press for the Institute of Commonwealth Studies.*

Freedom of Information Act 2017. Nassau, Bahamas: Government Publications.

Government of Bahamas (2018) *Proceeds of Crime Act 2018, Nasau, Bahamas.*

Inter-American Development Bank (2017) Project Completion Report: Investment Loan. *Project Name*: Modernization of The Barbados National Procurement System (BA- L1004).

The Grenada Authority for the Regulation of Financial Institutions Act, No.1 of 2008.

World Justice Project (2020) *Rule of Law Index.* World Justice Project. https://worldjusticeproject.org/sites/default/files/documents/WJP-ROLI-2020-Online_0.pdf

Legislations

Integrity in Public Life Act No. 24 of 2013

Audit Act No.26 of 1988

Procurement and Asset Disposal Act (2015)

Anti-Money Laundering Terrorist Financing Code, 2017

Anti-Terrorist Financing and Proliferation Act, 2015

Finance Administration Act, 2004

Financial Intelligence Unit Act, 2009

Prevention of Corruption Act, 2004

Proceeds of Crime Act, 2013

Chapter 2

The Bahamas

Lemarque A Campbell

Abstract

This study focuses on possible reasons why The Bahamas may be perceived as one of the least corrupt Commonwealth Caribbean countries by Transparency International's Corruption Perception Index. In this regard, it provides novel research and analysis on The Bahamas's anti-corruption initiatives, particularly on: (i) the legal and institutional frameworks that are aimed at mitigating corruption in the country; (ii) how groups such as the private sector, the media, civil society and international and regional organisations have contributed to anti-corruption efforts; (iii) some of the challenges that the country faces in its anti-corruption efforts; and (iv) how lessons from The Bahamas could be applied elsewhere in the Commonwealth Caribbean. The study is supported by a detailed analysis of both qualitative primary and secondary data sources, which include interviews conducted with senior government officials and representatives from external stakeholders. It concludes with recommendations to assist governments and other stakeholders seeking to enhance anti-corruption efforts in small island states.

1. Introduction

As part of the Commonwealth Secretariat's research into combatting corruption in the Caribbean, this section takes a closer look at The Bahamas and examines the possible reasons why the country has maintained relatively favourable scores on Transparency International's Corruption Perception Index (CPI). Table 1 illustrates that over the past five years, The Bahamas has remained among the top 30 perceived least corrupt countries in the world on the CPI.

Table 1. The Bahamas's Corruption Perception Index results (2016–2020)

Year	Score	World ranking
2016	66	24/176
2017	65	28/180
2018	65	29/180
2019	64	29/180
2020	63	30/180

The research that is presented here provides an analysis of: (i) the legal and institutional frameworks that are aimed at mitigating corruption in The Bahamas; (ii) how groups such as the private sector, the media, civil society and international and regional organisations have contributed to anti-corruption efforts in the country; (iii) some of the challenges that The Bahamas faces in its anti-corruption efforts; and iv) how the lessons learned could be applied elsewhere in the Commonwealth Caribbean.

2. Methodology

The first step in the research for this study was to obtain secondary data by reviewing existing literature, reports and legislation that relate to combating corruption in The Bahamas. Second, interviews were requested with senior officials and representatives from key government institutions, civil society organisations (CSOs) and international partners that are driving the anti-corruption initiatives in the country. This was done to validate the secondary data and to obtain further information required to fulfil the aims of the analysis.

Third, questionnaires were drafted to use during the interviews and examine the impact made by the key institutions involved in the fight against corruption; the extent to which the key factors and institutions have been able to facilitate a whole-of-government approach to combatting corruption; and how government institutions have worked with external stakeholders during their anti-corruption efforts.

Finally, extensive one-on-one interviews were conducted with seven senior officials and representatives from the identified government institutions, CSOs and international partners. Additionally, a focus group was held with three senior officials from the Office of the Attorney General and Ministry of Legal Affairs and the Office of the Director of Public Prosecutions. The one-on-one interviews and focus group were conducted via video conferences between 25 March and 23 April 2021.

3. Socio-Economic and Political Context

The Commonwealth of The Bahamas is made up of an extensive chain of over 700 islands and cays, of which 30 are inhabited, stretched across an archipelago in the Atlantic Ocean. It is located just 60 miles off the south-eastern coast of the US state of Florida and some 50 miles off the eastern tip of Cuba. Formerly a British colony, The Bahamas became independent on 10 July 1973.

Currently, The Bahamas has a population of nearly 400,000 people, most of whom are of African descent. There is a small but significant minority of mixed European and African heritage and a similar number of descendants of English pioneer settlers and loyalist refugees from the American Revolution. English is the official language. Due to the influx of Haitian immigrants since the mid-20th century, French or the related Haitian Creole vernacular have also emerged as spoken languages in the country.

The per capita gross domestic product (GDP) in The Bahamas has one of the highest in the region, with an economy heavily reliant on tourism and financial services. Tourism accounts for approximately 50 per cent of GDP and directly or indirectly employs half of the country's labour force. Most tourists come from the United States. In 2019, The Bahamas experienced a record-breaking number of over 7 million tourist arrivals.

Financial services constitute the second most important sector of the economy, accounting for about 15 per cent of GDP. Several hundred international banks and trust companies have been attracted to The Bahamas because there are no income or corporate taxes and because the secrecy of financial transactions is guaranteed. In recent years, financial services have been significantly impacted as international bodies considered the jurisdiction to be a tax haven and conduit for money laundering. Since 2017, the Government has made significant steps to improve the reputation of the country's financial services industry by enhancing the anti-money laundering regime and implementing all the necessary reforms to address international concerns regarding economic substance, preferential exemptions for foreign entities and lack of automatic exchange of tax information with other jurisdictions.

Manufacturing and agriculture combined contribute less than 7 per cent of GDP. Manufacturing industries centre on the production of rum and other liquor and also include cement, pharmaceuticals, canned fruits and frozen spiny lobster processing. Nearly all the country's foodstuffs are imported, largely from the United States, and the Bahamian dollar remains pegged to the US dollar.

As there are no income or corporate taxes, government revenue is heavily reliant on indirect taxes, such as customs duties on imported goods and value added tax. Recently, the Government has sought to manage an economy dealing with the dual, unprecedented economic crises wrought by the passage of Hurricane Dorian in September 2019, the worst natural disaster in the country's recorded history, and the effects of the global COVID-19 pandemic.

The Constitution of The Bahamas is based on the British Westminster model. There is a bicameral Parliament that comprises the House of Assembly and the Senate. The formal head of state is the British monarch, who is represented by a governor-general. The head of Government is the prime minister, who is formally appointed by the governor-general. The prime minister must be a member of the House of Assembly and must be able to command a majority of its votes. House members are elected by eligible voters – all citizens above the age of 18 – while members of the Senate are appointed by the governor-general on the advice of the prime minister and leader of the opposition. Currently, there are 39 elected Members of Parliament (MPs) and 16 appointed senators. The Bahamas has a multi-party system, predominantly led by the two major political parties: the Free National Movement (FNM) and the Progressive Liberal Party (PLP).

The FNM, led by Prime Minister Dr Hubert Minnis, won the last general election (10 May 2017) in a landslide: 35 out of the 39 parliamentary seats. Its campaign centred on anti-corruption, transparency and government accountability.

4. Legal and Institutional Backing for Anti-Corruption

The Bahamas signed the Inter-American Convention against Corruption (IACAC) on 2 June 1998 and ratified it on 9 March 2000. The IACAC is a regional convention that promotes and strengthens the development by each of the States Parties of the mechanisms needed to prevent, detect, punish and eradicate corruption. Additionally, The Bahamas became a party to the United Nations Convention against Corruption (UNCAC), the first global multilateral anti-corruption instrument, on 10 January 2008.

There is no single anti-corruption agency in The Bahamas. Instead, its anti-corruption framework spans across a compendium of laws and government institutions that work in tandem to reduce corruption in the country.

4.1 The legal system

The anti-corruption legal framework in The Bahamas includes the following primary laws that have been brought into force to date:

Penal Code (Ch. 84)

The *Penal Code* covers a wide spectrum of corruption offences, including the abuse of authority, active and passive bribery, corruption in the conduct of court proceedings, the sale of public offices and corruption during public elections. Every public officer who is found guilty of corruption, wilful oppression or extortion, in respect of their duties in office, commits a misdemeanour and would be liable to imprisonment for two years. Any person who corrupts or attempts to corrupt any public officer in respect of their duties would also be guilty of a misdemeanour. Charges were recently brought against three former politicians on extortion, under the Penal Code, and bribery, under the Prevention of Bribery Act, 1976 (see below for further details).

Commissions of Inquiry Act, 1911

The *Commissions of Inquiry Act* allows the governor-general to appoint a commission to inquire into and report on any matter stated as the subject of inquiry if he/she thinks it will be for the public benefit. Accordingly, it is possible for a commission to inquire into allegations of corruption involving public officials.

Powers and Privileges (Senate and House of Assembly) Act, 1969

This Act establishes certain bribery and conflicts of interest offences that pertain to senators and MPs in the conduct of their duties. The following offences are covered:

i.   any person who offers a bribe to influence the conduct of any senator or MP or offers a fee, compensation, gift or reward to any senator or MP for the promotion of or opposition to any draft legislation or matter before Parliament (*active bribery*); or

ii.   if any senator or MP accepts or agrees to accept a bribe or benefit of any kind for him/herself, or for any other person, for speaking, voting or refraining from a particular vote during parliamentary proceedings (*passive bribery*); or

iii. if any senator or MP brings forward or promotes in parliamentary proceedings any matter in which he/she may have acted for or receives a reward for (*conflicts of interest*).

These offences essentially address financial lobbying and the issues that arise with the principal-agent theory in corruption. An agency problem occurs where the politicians (agents) choose to engage in a corrupt transaction, in furtherance of their own interests and to the detriment of the interests of their constituents (principal) (Klitgaard, 1988;

Shleifer and Vishny, 1993). Therefore, when a politician, who has a primary duty to act on behalf of the overall public good for his/her constituents, can benefit by determining laws that serve the interest of a select few who can essentially 'buy' the politician, a conflict of interest exists and an offence is committed under this Act.

The Constitution, 1973

The Constitution disqualifies an individual from being appointed as a senator if he/she has an interest in any government contract and has not disclosed to the governor-general the nature of such contract and his/her interest in it. Additionally, a person would be disqualified from being elected as a member of the House of Assembly if he/she has an interest in any government contract and has not disclosed the nature of such contract and his/her interest in it by publishing a notice in the *Gazette* within one month before the day of election. These provisions have the potential to mitigate conflicts of interest among sitting parliamentarians.

Public Disclosure Act, 1976

Under the *Public Disclosure Act*, all MPs, senators and specified public officials are mandated to annually submit a statutory declaration form of their financial disclosures to the Public Disclosure Commission (the Commission), with particulars detailing their assets, income and liabilities. Additionally, the financial disclosure must also cover particulars on the assets, income and liabilities for the declarant's spouse and children (over the age of 18). Significant emphasis is thus put on monitoring the financial affairs of those required to disclose under the Act to discover and mitigate instances of illicit enrichment.

The Commission must examine every statutory declaration form that is submitted and may request any additional information or explanation that would assist in the examination of the declaration. Once the Commission is satisfied, after examination, that a declaration form submitted by a parliamentarian has been fully made, it is then mandated to publish a summary of that declaration in the official Government *Gazette*.

Offences under the Act include:

  i.   failure, without reasonable cause, to submit a required statutory declaration in accordance with the provisions of the Act;

  ii. knowingly making any false statement in statutory declarations;

  iii. failure, without reasonable cause, to provide additional information or explanation as may be requested by the Commission; and

  iv. failure, without reasonable cause, to attend an enquiry being conducted by the Commission, or knowingly giving any false information during such enquiry.

Any person who commits any of the offences would be liable to a fine of up to US$10,000.00 and/or to imprisonment for a term of up to two years. Additionally, where the offence involves the deliberate non-disclosure of property, the court must, in addition to imposing a fine and/or term of imprisonment, declare that the property be forfeited to the Government; or make an order for an amount equivalent to the assessed value of such property to be paid to the Government.

Prevention of Bribery Act, 1976 (the Bribery Act)

The Bribery Act establishes offences against any individual found bribing a public official/civil servant (active bribery), as well as any public official/civil servant who accepts such bribes (passive bribery).

This Act, in conjunction with provisions under the Penal Code, was used two months after the Minnis administration came into office in May 2017, when two former cabinet ministers and a former senator was brought before the courts on charges of bribery and extortion. This was viewed as a societal shift, as it was the first time in a long time that Bahamians witnessed politicians being formally charged with corruption. Lambsdorff (2015) regards the most important factor in fighting corruption, both in the private and the public sector, to be the tone at the top. The anti-corruption tone being set by Prime Minister Minnis is therefore especially important, given that followers tend to react to the messages sent by their leader more than any monetary incentive, as found in an experiment by d'Adda, Copper and Weber (2014).

Parliamentary Elections Act, 1992 (the Elections Act)

The Elections Act covers corruption offences undertaken during public elections, in particular the bribery of voters by politicians and their agents as well as bribes solicited by voters themselves. Any person found guilty of a bribery offence under the Elections Act would be liable to: (i) imprisonment for a term of up to two years; or (ii) a fine not exceeding $2,000.00; or (iii) both. Additionally, the convicted individual would be barred from registering as a voter, voting at an election or being elected as a MP for a period of seven years.

Financial Administration and Audit Act, 2010

This Act addresses matters in which public officers fail to collect any money owed to the Government, the improper payment of public monies or any payment of such monies that is not duly vouched. In these instances, the Financial Secretary may surcharge against the public officer the loss or a lesser amount as he/she determines. The Act also establishes a government tender board that deals with contracts valued between US$50,000 and US$250,000.

Freedom of Information Act, 2017 (FOIA)

The FOIA provides the public with a general right to access information held by government authorities. However, most of its provisions, including the actual process of applying for and accessing information, have not been brought into force to date. Once the FOIA is fully in force, the public can request all information held by the Government, except for documents that are exempt such as those containing information regarding private citizens or information deemed classified for reasons of national security. Therefore, the FOIA will provide a mechanism to reinforce and give further effect to certain fundamental principles for a stronger democracy:

government accountability and transparency and public participation in the national decision-making process.

One significant FOIA provision that was brought into force in 2018 is the whistle-blower provision in section 47. Whistleblowing is regarded as a highly effective anti-corruption and democratic accountability mechanism that may lead to widespread reforms, enhancing the quality of life for society at large. Whistleblowing provides people with the means to come forward and report corrupt practices that are affecting organisations or society, thereby giving the relevant authorities access to the information they need to fulfil their mandates. Mansbach (2011, p.13) found that: 'By disclosing wrongdoing that results in public harm, all the forms of whistleblowing protect the community, promote the public good, and extend the rule of law'.

Financial Transactions Reporting Act, 2018 (FTRA)

The Government enacted the FTRA in response to the Mutual Evaluation Report of the Caribbean Financial Action Task Force (CFATF) in July 2017, which identified substantial gaps in The Bahamas's legal and regulatory regime relating to anti-money laundering/combating the financing of terrorism (AML/CFT). The Act imposes mandatory obligations on financial institutions operating in the country to: (i) verify the identity of existing and prospective customers and clients, including ultimate beneficial owners; (ii) maintain verification and transaction records for prescribed periods; and (iii) report suspicious transactions that might involve the proceeds of criminal conduct to the Financial Intelligence Unit (FIU).

Register of Beneficial Ownership Act, 2018 (RBOA)

The RBOA provides for the Attorney-General to establish a secure search system of databases that are maintained by registered agents in The Bahamas. Every registered agent must enter and continue to update as necessary particulars into its database regarding the beneficial ownership of each legal entity, i.e., Bahamian incorporated company, that it is responsible for. The databases must be accessible to appointed officials from the Office of the Attorney-General, who have subscribed to an Oath of Confidentiality, through a secure search system.

This is a further advancement to anti-corruption efforts in the country, as the RBOA could serve as an invaluable tool in the investigation of money laundering or corruption matters, where illicit proceeds are transferred to or held by Bahamian companies.

Proceeds of Crime Act, 2018 (POCA)

The POCA strengthens measures to recover the proceeds and property used, or intended to be used, for criminal offences and to combat identified risks such as corruption and money laundering. It provides law enforcement agencies with wider powers when it comes to seizures and forfeitures relative to the proceeds of crime. Ms Abigail Farrington, Senior Counsel in the Office of the Director of Public Prosecutions (ODPP), indicated that, 'the enactment of the POCA has significantly increased the ODPP's ability to investigate, detect and confiscate the proceeds of crime'.

The impact that the POCA has had on money laundering and corruption matters is indicated in the statistics: While there was only one charge and prosecution for money laundering between 2015 and 2016, by 2018, 82 individuals had been brought before the courts on money laundering, fraud and corruption charges, which led to approximately 30 convictions. And as of March 2021, there were 224 money-laundering charges and 61 convictions.

A notable aspect of the POCA is the introduction of Unexplained Wealth Orders, which provide the Director of Public Prosecutions with a mechanism to apply to the Court to enquire into the finances of an individual charged with a specified offence, such as bribery, money laundering or misconduct in public office. The Court may make an Unexplained Wealth Order *absolute,* requiring the person charged to pay a specified amount to the Crown, if it is satisfied on the balance of probabilities that any part of the charged person's wealth was not lawfully obtained or held. The specified amount that the charged person would have to pay is the amount that the Crown is satisfied does not represent his/her lawfully acquired property (the 'unexplained wealth amount'). What makes these Orders a game changer is that the burden of proof would be on the charged individual, instead of the prosecution, to prove that his/her wealth is lawfully acquired.

Fiscal Responsibility Act, 2018

The objectives of this Act are to:

i.   establish the principles and procedures of responsible fiscal management;

ii.   guide the formulation and implementation of the fiscal objectives;

iii.   guide the annual budget within a medium-term fiscal framework; and

iv.   facilitate effective parliamentary and public scrutiny of the fiscal performance of the Government.

This Act aims to improve transparency in the management of public finances and establishes an independent oversight and enforcement body called the Fiscal Responsibility Council (see below for details). This important piece of legislation reshapes the culture of public accountability by enabling more parliamentary and public scrutiny of the fiscal management and performance of the Government.

4.2 The institutional framework

In addition to the legislation that have been brought into force to date, the following institutions provide the primary backing for The Bahamas's anti-corruption framework:

The Royal Bahamas Police Force (RBPF) Complaints and Corruption Unit

This unit is mandated to identify and investigate all alleged cases of dishonesty and unethical behaviour made by members of the public against members of the RBPF. It must submit a progress report of the work undertaken, at the end of every quarter, to the Police Inspectorate and the Commissioner of Police.

RBPF Anti-Corruption Unit

This unit was established soon after the Minnis administration took office in 2017, with a mandate to investigate and prosecute persons accused of corruption, theft and various forms of misappropriation throughout the public sector.

Office of the Director of Public Prosecutions (ODPP)

The ODPP has a general responsibility to initiate the prosecution of criminal offences, including corruption-related offences. A significant advance was made on 11 June 2018, when the DPP became a constitutionally independent position with a five-year tenure. According to Prime Minister Minnis, 'this historic occasion marked an important advancement in good governance and democracy in the country; hopefully, any suggestion of political influence over prosecutions by the Executive arm of Government will now be a thing of the past' (Thompson, 2018). Before this position was guaranteed its independence, public prosecutions in criminal matters were instituted under the instructions of the Attorney-General, a politician and member of the Executive.

In recent years, the ODPP has created a specialised unit related to the proceeds of crime and money laundering. Currently, the unit has eight assigned prosecutors, who collaborate with the RBPF's Anti-Corruption Unit, to enhance detection, investigation and the prosecution of money laundering, fraud and corruption offences.

Office of the Attorney General (OAG) and Ministry of Legal Affairs

The OAG ensures that the Government is complying with its international obligations under the UNCAC and IACAC. As the legal advisor to the Government, it is responsible for drafting and preparing legislation and guaranteeing that this does not breach the Constitution. In terms of anti-corruption work, the OAG continuously monitors whether corrupt practices are being conducted and the various offences that go along with them. It also maintains relationships with its international counterparts in providing mutual legal assistance for the purpose of gathering and exchanging information to enforce anti-corruption laws.

Judiciary

The judiciary is headed by a Chief Justice. The legal system in The Bahamas is based on English common law. Judicial power on the islands resides in the magistrates' courts, the Supreme Court and Court of Appeal, with the ultimate court of appeal being the Judicial Committee of the Privy Council in the United Kingdom. The Bahamian judiciary is predominantly independent, and there have been no major reports in recent years of attempts by powerful figures to use political or other influence to secure favourable rulings (Freedom House, 2020). To further support this claim, the judiciary was regarded as the least corrupt public institution, among all assessed Bahamian government institutions, in the 2020 World Justice Project Rule of Law Index.

Auditor-General

The Auditor-General is responsible for examining, enquiring into and auditing the accounts of all accounting officers and individuals responsible for the collection, receipt, custody or disposal of public monies and reporting any irregularities. Through its reports, the Auditor-General's office reveals any problematic issues regarding government revenue and expenditures and recommends ways to improve the management of public finances.

The public maintains a considerable level of trust in the Auditor-General's office to unearth corrupt activities in the management of public finances. 'Without any official whistleblowing channels, I continuously receive tips by the public, where citizens would either call or write me to provide information regarding the mismanagement of public finances, and sometimes these tips are used to corroborate existing information regarding government corruption', said Mr Terrance Bastian, Auditor-General.

Public Accounts Committee

The Manual of Procedure in the Business of the House of Assembly provides for a Committee of Public Accounts to be established for the examination of the accounts showing appropriation of the sums granted by the legislature to meet public expenditure. It is mandatory that this Committee report at least once every session. The Committee is dominated by members of the opposition party.

Public Disclosure Commission

This Commission is established under the *Public Disclosure Act, 1976* and is mandated to receive and examine the annual financial declarations, containing particulars of assets, income and liabilities, submitted by MPs, senators and senior public officials.

Financial Intelligence Unit (FIU)

The FIU is responsible for receiving and analysing suspicious transaction reports (e.g., reports on suspected money laundering offences) that are generated by financial institutions and distributing them to the Commissioner of Police.

The National Crime Intelligence Agency

This Agency is established under the *National Crime Intelligence Agency Act, 2019* to collect information and intelligence relating to threats to the security of The Bahamas. It also coordinates intelligence gathering and joint strategic planning among the various law enforcement agencies and government departments and effective networking between regional and international partners. Public sector corruption and money laundering are among the offences on which the agency is mandated to collect intelligence.

Identified Risk Framework Steering Committee

This Committee is established under section 6 of the POCA and comprises 13 members who represent a wide spectrum of government agencies that are relevant to the fight against money laundering and corruption in The Bahamas.

The objectives of this Committee, among others, are to:

i.   periodically coordinate a national risk assessment to identify, assess and understand the identified risk in the country;

ii. coordinate the development, regular review and implementation of national policies and activities designed to mitigate the identified risk; and

iii. establish appropriate mechanisms to provide information on the identified risk to relevant financial institutions, self-regulatory bodies and professional associations.

Section 2 of the POCA defines identified risk as corruption and money laundering, among others.

Since 2017, the Committee has been meeting at least once per week to focus on common issues, emerging risks and risk containment by examining procedures, policies, legislation, guidelines and government structures. As a result of the Committee's hard work, The Bahamas was successfully removed from the Financial Action Task Force's (FATF) grey list in 2020. Countries on the FATF grey list represent a much higher risk of money laundering and terrorism financing.

This Committee takes a coordinated approach by bringing together the relevant government agencies and regulators to establish 'collective action' initiatives to mitigate identified risk. According to Ms Kenrah Newry, Assistant Director of Legal Affairs in the Office of the Attorney General, 'In the past, it was always difficult for domestic regulators to talk to each other as there was a territorial wall created between them. However, efforts have been made to break down these walls and relative authorities are now working as a cohesive whole, as opposed to working in silos.'

Accordingly, this initiative helps to combat the issues presented by the collective action theory of corruption, i.e., where an institutional or organisational culture of corruption leads to the normalisation of corrupt practices at a societal as well as individual level, and to impunity for violating or ignoring formal anti-corruption rules (Appolloni and Nshombo, 2014).

Digital Transformation Unit (DTU)

The DTU was established in the Office of the Prime Minister to manage the Digital Transformation to Strengthen Competitiveness Programme (the 'Digital Project'), launched on 13 November 2019. 'The Office of the Prime Minister has taken ownership of the project', said Ms Damara Dillett, Legal Specialist in The Office. The fact that this project is being championed by senior government officials sets the tone at the top, ensuring that there is widespread buy-in among the various government agencies.

The Digital Project supports a whole-of-government approach to combatting corruption. 'The intention is for every Government Ministry to become fully digitised, thereby improving the ease of doing business, enhancing government efficiency and ultimately reducing corruption', said the Hon. Elsworth Johnson, Minister of Financial Services, Trade and Industry and Immigration. The Project will make it possible for all major government services to be accessed online, thereby increasing the transparency of government activities and strengthening auditing and control mechanisms. Its main aim is to remove delays and 'red tape' that citizens and business interests encounter when doing business with the Government.

As a part of the Digital Project, the Government launched the MyGateway portal, which is a centralised online platform to request and pay for a range of government services. Currently, there are eight services connected to the portal but the aim is for 200 to be onboarded there over a five-year period. As it relates to direct anti-corruption measures, another aspect of the Digital Project focuses on providing the Government with technical support for the implementation of the FOIA.

The DTU also works closely with the various government ministries, departments and agencies in a collaborative manner that is fully facilitated and supported through the Office of the Prime Minister and formalised through memorandums of understanding. Ms Dillett further stated that, 'efforts are currently being made to develop a 'whole-of-government' digital transformation collaborative policy document, so that every government entity can share in the vision of digital transformation.'

The benefits of moving towards digitisation in The Bahamas not only include greater efficiency but also provide the country with an opportunity to digitise reporting and enhance data analytics, which will increase transparency and accountability in the provision of government services. 'This project will essentially reduce opportunities for public officials who stray away from processes and engage in corruption', said the Hon. K. Peter Turnquest, former Deputy Prime Minister and Minister of Finance. He further noted that,

> 'It was recognised that the less contact customers have with government officials and civil servants, the less likely it is that you're going to have corrupt activity. Increased digitisation has reduced the physical handling of cash by civil servants, which has provided positive results so far. For example, customs revenue has increased in terms of the yield. Overall, the system of internal control has been strengthened, such that there is a lot more transparency in the system. And the grievance process is a lot more transparent and accessible.'

5. The Private Sector, Media and Civil Society

5.1 The private sector

In recent years, the Government has made a concerted effort to consult with industry leaders and private sector organisations on draft legislation that relates to anti-corruption reforms. Consultations are usually held before the draft legislation is tabled in Parliament for debate. The Government has also invited numerous private sector bodies to participate and present during the UNCAC and IACAC country review processes.

The private sector maintains a close relationship with the Ministry of Finance. The Ministry frequently holds stakeholder meetings with the business community where there is a dialogue maintained to talk about the issues affecting the management of public finances. The Hon. K. Peter Turnquest, former Deputy Prime Minister and Minister of Finance, expressed that: 'individuals will raise issues in that closed setting that they may not want to raise in the public, which provides the Ministry with clues as to where maladministration is occurring.'

The private sector also plays a pivotal role in ensuring that the Government is being fiscally responsible in its use of taxpayers' money and not overspending through practices such as corruption. The *Fiscal Responsibility Act, 2018* (see above) establishes the Fiscal Responsibility Council, which is an independent private sector body, comprised of five members with legal, business, economic, accounting and financial backgrounds. The Council members are appointed by the governor-general upon the nomination of the Bahamas Bar Association, the Bahamas Chamber of Commerce and Employers Confederation, the University of The Bahamas, the Bahamas Institute of Chartered Accountants and the Chartered Financial Analyst Society of The Bahamas.

The Council submits annual reports to Parliament assessing the Government's budgetary discipline. It reviews and assesses the Government's Fiscal Strategy Report, Mid-Year Review, Annual Budget and audited annual accounts.

5.2 The media

Press freedom in The Bahamas is constitutionally guaranteed and generally respected in practice. Privately owned newspapers and radio broadcasters freely express a variety of views (Freedom House, 2020). Additionally, people can freely express personal views in private and in public without fear of retribution or surveillance (ibid.). Talk radio is extremely popular, promotes dialogue and allows citizens to express themselves on many national issues.

The media play an active role in exposing corruption matters. For example, in 2017, investigative journalists broke the story, without reprisal, of a sitting Cabinet Minister who had directly solicited commercial contracts from a foreign developer for his own businesses (The Tribune, 2017). Additionally, the media frequently takes the Government to task by reporting on non-compliance with relevant anti-corruption laws, such as the *Public Disclosure Act*. For example, according to Virgil (2016a, 2016b), most parliamentarians still had not filed their 2015 financial declarations by the end of April 2016, almost two months after the filing deadline.

5.3 Civil society

The Government has developed a number of consultative channels with leading civil society organisations (CSOs). For example, the Ministry of Finance has engaged extensively with CSOs (and the private sector) in its development of legislation to enhance the management of public finances, while the Office of the Attorney-General (OAG) maintains an open dialogue with them. Meetings are held periodically at the OAG's office, where civil society representatives are invited to discuss various draft legislation and legal reforms, such as the Integrity Commission Bill and the Ombudsman Bill, directly with the Attorney-General. In 2018, the OAG hosted and invited CSOs to training sessions on how the FOIA would work in practice.

Additionally, the OAG ensures representatives from various CSOs are invited to meet and provide presentations to external officials during the UNCAC and IACAC on-site review processes. That way civil society representatives can provide objective information and knowledge of potential difficulties in the Government's efforts to implement these conventions.

The Organization for Responsible Governance (ORG) is currently the leading CSO in The Bahamas advocating for anti-corruption reforms and good governance. Mr Matthew Aubry, its Executive Director, expressed that ORG has been involved with the Government in various legislative consultations on anti-corruption reforms. The ORG has been invited to provide comments on draft legislation, such as the Fiscal Responsibility Bill, the Public Procurement Bill and the Public Finance Management Bill.

The ORG also maintains a working relationship with the Ministry of National Security. Some initiatives include a discussion on establishing greater integrity at the community level through collaboration with various neighbourhood watch groups. Additionally, Mr Aubry was appointed as a CSO representative for the Police Inspectorate, an advisory group, mandated to meet quarterly, that reports to the Minister on matters relating to police corruption complaints. Additional members on the Police Inspectorate include the CEO and Executive Director of the Bahamas Financial Services Board and two retired police officers.

In addition to the Police Inspectorate, Mr Aubry has been invited to serve on various government committees established in the wake of COVID-19, including asco-chair of the National Coordination Committee, the Economic Recovery Committee and the Food Distribution Task Force. According to Mr Aubry: 'These appointments were not only made to recognise the need for greater civil society representation in government processes, but also ensure that there is a voice at the table advocating for accountability measures as the Government seeks to implement COVID-19 recovery initiatives.'

6. International/Regional Organisations

The following are examples of international and regional organisations with which the Government collaborates on initiatives to assist in its anti-corruption efforts:

6.1 Organization of American States (OAS)

The Government participates in the Follow-Up Mechanism for the Implementation of the IACAC (MESICIC), which is the Anti-Corruption Mechanism of the OAS. The

MESICIC brings together 33 of the 34 Member States to review their anti-corruption legal frameworks and institutions. In this regard, OAS officials regularly conduct on-site visits to The Bahamas, where they meet with government officials and civil society representatives to obtain objective information and better knowledge of potential difficulties in the implementation of the IACAC. The OAS also provides The Bahamas with anti-corruption technical assistance.

6.2 Commonwealth Secretariat

The Commonwealth Secretariat has provided technical assistance to The Bahamas in the drafting of various pieces of legislation pertaining to anti-corruption efforts, such as the recently passed *Public Debt Management Act, 2021*. The Bahamas is also part of the Commonwealth Caribbean Association of Integrity Commissions and Anti-Corruption Bodies, an initiative established by the Commonwealth Secretariat to create dialogue among Commonwealth Caribbean countries on issues regarding the fight against corruption.

6.3 Inter-American Development Bank (IDB)

The Government's Digital Project is funded by a US$30 million loan from the Inter-American Development Bank (IDB). The IDB also provides overall support to the Project through its subject matter experts, along with regional and sub-regional liaisons.

6.4 U.S. Department of State

Due to its proximity, The Bahamas maintains a close relationship with the United States. The U.S. Department of State, through its International Narcotics and Law Enforcement Affairs (INL) office at the U.S. Embassy in The Bahamas, has provided the Government with foreign assistance in furtherance of its transparency and anti-corruption efforts (U.S. Embassy in The Bahamas, 2018). This assistance includes financial support, in the amount of US$1.4 million, that was provided to the Government in 2018.

As a part of the 2018 funding, the U.S. Department of State engaged the International Development Law Organization (IDLO), an intergovernmental organisation dedicated to the rule of law, to develop and implement a project to assist the Government in its efforts to mitigate corruption. IDLO is mandated to provide technical assistance to prosecutors in the handling of corruption matters and in the development of anti-corruption policies. For this project, IDLO reports directly to the Office of the Prime Minster.

Additionally, the Ministry of National Security has engaged a reputable US company in a consultancy contract, in partnership with the U.S. Department of State, to increase the capacity development for intelligence gathering on financial crimes and asset tracing matters.

7. Conclusion: Challenges, Lessons and Recommendations

7.1 Challenges

The Bahamas currently faces the following challenges in its anti-corruption framework and efforts:

1. There is no framework regulating the financing of political parties and candidates running for elected office. In both its 2012 and 2017 Electoral Observation Mission reports on elections in The Bahamas, the OAS recommended that the Government implement campaign finance laws (Turnquest, 2017). In this regard, a 2017 national survey found that: 41 per cent of Bahamians believe that voters are always bribed in Bahamian elections; a majority of people agreed that money has a greater influence in politics than in the past; and an overwhelming 76 per cent agreed that wealthy individuals often use their influence on Government for their own interests and there needs to be stricter rules to prevent this (Campbell, 2018). Perhaps because of such views, 74 per cent of respondents believed that there should be limits on campaign spending during Bahamian elections (ibid).

2. There is no law or clear policy in place to address the 'revolving door' – the movement of individuals between public office and private sector while working on the same sector issue – which may result in conflicts of interest and in former public officials misusing the information and power they hold to benefit private interests.

3. *The Public Disclosure Act, 1976* requires all MPs, senators and senior officials to disclose their assets, income and liabilities to the Public Disclosure Commission on an annual basis. However, some parliamentarians have repeatedly failed to disclose over several years and there has not been one recorded criminal action against offenders.

4. The Bahamas enacted its first whistle-blower protection law in March 2018. The new law prohibits retaliation against those who report in good faith information that would disclose wrongdoing, including corruption and maladministration. However, this legal prohibition on retaliation against whistle-blowers was not accompanied by the creation of any new reporting channels, with prospective whistle-blowers still expected to report possible corruption and maladministration to the police. This is an unappealing option for many would-be whistle-blowers, given that Bahamian citizens perceive the police as the most corrupt public service in the country (Campbell, 2018). In addition to the lack of trustworthy independent reporting channels, there are numerous other deficiencies, including a lack of anonymity and confidentiality protections and an absence of measures to ensure that whistle-blower complaints receive adequate follow-up.

5. The Bahamas is a small country with very close-knit communities and a political system substantially based on patronage networks and familial ties. In this regard, the Hon. Marvin Dames, Minister of National Security, indicated that: 'this could breed some very negative activities; for example, in the award of government contracts to close ties, or immunity from laws or policies that

should be applied across the board'. The lack of economic opportunities for most Bahamians means that seeking political patronage through a party machine may seem like the only way to ensure economic security or advancement. Systems like this – characterised by extensive patronage networks fortified by strong social and familial ties among the governing elite – are especially inhospitable to whistle-blowers.

6. Under Section 315 of the Bahamas Penal Code, the law criminalises both negligent and intentional libel, with a penalty of six months' imprisonment for the former and two years for the latter. This legal provision may threaten or undermine the ability of civil society actors to uncover and report on all forms of corruption and to hold leaders accountable.

7. There are no competition/antitrust laws in The Bahamas. Therefore, there is no prohibition on hard-core cartels or collusion established between companies.

7.2 Lessons

Based on the analysis in this study, the following lessons are among the key factors that may have led to The Bahamas being perceived as an anti-corruption leader within the Commonwealth Caribbean:

1. It maintains a robust legislative and institutional anti-corruption framework. Currently, there are over 13 pieces of legislation that have been brought into force, covering a range of offences, along with over 11 institutions that provide the backing for the anti-corruption framework. Notably, the Government has made significant steps in ensuring that the country's anti-money laundering regime is brought to an acceptable international standard.

2. It is generally perceived as a highly free country, scoring 91 out of 100 in the 2020 Freedom in the World Report (Freedom House, 2020). Some of the acknowledged freedoms include an independent judiciary and prosecution, which are not perceived as being subject to political interference. Additionally, the Constitution provides for freedom of expression, including for the press, and the Government generally respects this right.

3. Anti-corruption initiatives are being led by the Office of the Prime Minister, setting the 'tone at the top'.

4. The Government has taken a holistic approach to combatting corruption and money laundering, where government agencies collaborate in collective action initiatives to mitigate corruption risks.

5. The Government maintains strong engagement with civil society, the private sector and international and regional partners in its anti-corruption efforts.

6. The Government has incorporated its anti-corruption efforts into broader national development initiatives, which is evident in the movement towards increased digitisation of public services.

7. The Government has increased the level of transparency in the management of public finances.

7.3 Recommendations

Based on the analysis presented in this study, the following recommendations are made:

1. Governments should seek to incorporate anti-corruption reforms into larger reforms for national development, such as enhancing the ease of doing business or increasing government efficiency, as this will ensure greater support from the citizenry.

2. Once a country maintains a robust anti-corruption legal and institutional framework, this will assist in fighting corruption even if it does not have a primary anti-corruption agency.

3. It is fundamental for anti-corruption initiatives to be championed by a senior government official, such as the Prime Minister, to ensure that there is greater buy-in among government agencies.

4. Governments should enact effective political campaign finance legislation to ensure that political parties frequently report their finances, including all donations received and expenditures, to an independent election authority. Additionally, they should establish a cap on political campaign spending to limit the influence that money has during elections.

5. It is important for all relevant government agencies to collaborate on anti-corruption initiatives in a collective action approach.

6. It is vital for government agencies to engage with the private sector, civil society and international and regional partners in their anti-corruption efforts, as this will increase both the credibility of these efforts and trust in the government.

7. To address the 'revolving door' challenge, governments should ensure that a 'cooling off' period is implemented and enforced in which there is a specified period before senior government officials are allowed to move into private sector entities that they had oversight of. Otherwise, too many questions arise regarding potential conflicts of interest, which would continue to erode public trust in government.

8. Governments should ensure that the judiciary and prosecution remain independent and free from political influence.

9. The media and civil society should be guaranteed freedom of expression in practice.

Bibliography

Appolloni, A and JM Mushagalusa Nshombo (2014) 'Public Procurement and Corruption in Africa: A Literature Review'. In: Decarolis, F and M Fray (eds), *Public Procurement's Place in the World: The Charge towards Sustainability and Innovation*, 185–208. Basingstoke, UK: Palgrave McMillan.

Campbell, L (2018) 'Global Corruption Barometer: The Bahamas'. Nassau: Citizens for a Better Bahamas.

d'Adda, G, D Darai and RA Weber (2014) 'Do Leaders Affect Ethical Conduct?' Working Paper No. 167. Zurich: Department of Economics, University of Zurich.

Freedom House (2020) *Freedom in The World 2020: The Bahamas.* Freedom House. https://freedomhouse.org/country/bahamas/freedom-world/2020

Gambetta, D (2009) *Codes of the Underworld: How Criminals Communicate.* Princeton, NJ: Princeton University Press.

Klitgaard, R (1988) *Controlling Corruption.* Oakland, CA: University of California Press.

Lambsdorff, G (2015) 'Preventing Corruption by Promoting Trust: Insights from Behavioral Science'. Faculty of Business and Economics Working Paper, December. Passau, Germany: University of Passau.

Manandhar, N (2014) *Anti-Corruption Strategies: Understanding What Works, What Doesn't and Why? Lessons learned from the Asia-Pacific Region.* Bangkok: United Nations Development Programme (UNDP). https://www1.undp.org/content/dam/undp/library/Democratic%20Governance/Anti-corruption/UNDP%20ACS%20Asia%20Pacific%20%20Anti-corruption%20Strategies.pdf

Mansbach, A (2011) 'Whistleblowing as Fearless Speech: The Radical Democratic Effects of Late Modern Parrhesia'. In: Lewis, D. and W. Vandekerckhove (eds), *Whistleblowing and Democratic Values*, 12–26. International Whistleblowing Research Network.

Organization of American States (1996) *Inter-American Convention against Corruption* (B-58). 29 March.

Shleifer, A and RW Vishny (1993) 'Corruption'. *The Quarterly Journal of Economics* 108(3): 599–617.

The Tribune (2017) 'Tribune Exclusive: Fitzgerald Sought Millions From Baha Mar'. *The Tribune*, 20 April. http://www.tribune242.com/news/2017/apr/20/fitzgerald-sought-millions-baha-mar/

Thompson, L (2018) 'Appointment of Independent DPP a Sign of Good Governance, Says Prime Minister'. *Bahamas Local*, 13 June. https://www.bahamaslocal.com/newsitem/199368/Appointment_of_Independent_DPP_a_sign_of_good_governance_says_Prime_Minister.html

Turnquest, A (2017) 'Observers Point to Lack of Technology in Election'. *The Tribune*, 12 May. http://www.tribune242.com/news/2017/may/12/observers-point-lack-technology-election/

United Nations General Assembly (2003) *United Nations Convention against Corruption.* A/RES/58/4, 31 October.

U.S. Embassy in The Bahamas, 2018. *Remarks: U.S. Presents The Bahamas Government with $1.4M for Anti-Corruption Efforts.* Nassau: U.S. Embassy in The Bahamas. https://bs.usembassy.gov/remarks-u-s-presents-the-bahamas-Government-with-1-4m-for-anti-corruption-efforts/

Virgil, K (2016a) 'Gray Defends Bamsi Contract for Former PLP Minister'. *The Tribune*, 16 February. http://www.tribune242.com/news/2016/feb/16/gray-defends-bamsi-contract-former-plp-minister/

Virgil, K (2016b) 'The MPs Who Failed to Disclose'. *The Tribune*, 25 April. http://www.tribune242.com/news/2016/apr/25/mps-who-failed-disclose/

World Justice Project (2020) *Rule of Law Index*. World Justice Project. https://worldjusticeproject.org/sites/default/files/documents/WJP-ROLI-2020-Online_0.pdf

Legislation

Commissions of Inquiry Act 1911

Constitution 1973

Financial Administration and Audit Act 2010

Financial Transactions Reporting Act 2018

Fiscal Responsibility Act 2018

Freedom of Information Act 2017

National Crime Intelligence Agency Act 2019

Parliamentary Elections Act 1992

Penal Code (c.84)

Police Force Act 2009

Powers and Privileges (Senate and House of Assembly) Act 1969

Prevention of Bribery Act 1976

Proceeds of Crime Act 2018

Public Disclosure Act 1976 (c.9)

Register of Beneficial Ownership Act 2018

Interviews

Hon. Marvin Dames, M P and Minister of National Security (conducted 23 April 2021).

Hon. Elsworth Johnson, MP and Minister of Financial Services, Trade and Industry and Immigration (conducted 19 April 2021).

Ms Damara Dillett, Legal Specialist, Digital Transformation Unit, The Office of the Prime Minister (conducted 31 March 2021).

Dr Cassandra Nottage, National Identified Risk Framework Coordinator, OAG and Ministry of Legal Affairs (conducted 30 March 2021).

Ms Michelle Dean, Assistant Director of Legal Affairs, OAG and Ministry of Legal Affairs (conducted 30 March 2021).

Ms Kenrah Newry, Assistant Director of Legal Affairs, OAG and Ministry of Legal Affairs (conducted 30 March 2021).

Ms Abigail Farrington, Senior Counsel, ODPP (conducted 30 March 2021).

Mr Matthew Aubry, Executive Director, ORG (conducted 26 March 2021).

Hon. K. Peter Turnquest, MP and former Deputy Prime Minister and Minister of Finance (2017–2020) (conducted 25 March 2021).

Mr Terrance Bastian, Auditor-General (conducted 25 March 2021).

Chapter 3

Barbados

Dirk Harrison

Abstract

Barbados has maintained a consistently high score on Transparency International's Corruption Perceptions Index (CPI) over the past 10 years. It has made significant progress in combatting the problem, unlike some of its counterpart countries in the region. This report highlights and analyses the anti-corruption framework in the country and examines a multiplicity of elements, including the anti-corruption drivers over the past 10 years. There exists a primary legal and institutional framework for combatting corruption and there is a culture of discipline and the maintenance of the rule of law. Barbadians have a strong sense of nationalism and high levels of social order, and the roles of the police and the education system have in a significant way defined the attributes of self-discipline, honesty and orderliness. However, the Government ought to fast track the implementation of a single anti-corruption regime. Countries within the region should consider implementing more robust public education strategies within the anti-corruption framework through a whole-of-community approach where multiple stakeholders are engaged, especially the youth. The main thrust of the public education strategy must be to reinforce the attributes of self-discipline, honesty and the maintenance of law and order.

1. Introduction

1.1 Background and purpose

This report highlights and analyses the anti-corruption framework in Barbados and examines a multiplicity of elements that have helped it make significant progress in combatting the problem. The country is considered an 'island of success' in terms of the its ability to reduce the prevalence of corruption, although it continues to experience challenges.

According to Transparency International's Corruption Perceptions Index (CPI), Barbados has consistently ranked as the least corrupt country in the region over the past 10 years (see Table 1). This report examines the legal and institutional framework as well as the role of the private sector, media, civil society and international/regional organisations. It attempts to capture the factors and institutions contributing to the reduction of the impact of corruption and the elements that have enabled Barbados to implement successful anti-corruption strategies. The findings culminate with lessons learnt, challenges and recommendations that can guide the region's anti-corruption efforts.

Barbados has signed and ratified the Inter-American Convention against Corruption (ICAC) and has signed but not ratified the United Nations' Convention against Corruption (UNCAC). Importantly, UNCAC advances that State parties should strive to:

> 'enhance their cooperation at various levels with developing countries, with a view to strengthening the capacity of the latter to prevent and combat corruption. Conveniently, the UNCAC itself provides an internationally agreed framework for organizing such efforts. A framework, however, should not be confused with a blue-print. There is no single model of reform; instead, leadership in each country must determine priorities and the appropriate sequencing of steps towards implementation' (UNCAC, 2007).

Hinds (2019), Smith and Larimer (2018) and Weible and Sabatier (2017) share the notion of a non-governmental public action and advocacy coalition framework/ issue networks perspective. Their underlying argument is that citizens, too, have the right to lobby for or against what is right or wrong. A sense of responsibility within the community or being your 'brother's or sister's keeper', is one reason for taking public action. This principle is relevant to the findings since most of the participants attributed Barbados' consistently high ranking and scores from the CPI to the country's cultural fabric and values as well as to its laws and regulations.

1.2 Transparency International's Corruption Perceptions Index (CPI)

The CPI is the most cited corruption index (Hawthorne, 2012). Countries such as New Zealand (ranked 1, scored 88), Denmark (ranked 1, scored 88), Finland (ranked 2, scored 85), Switzerland (ranked 3, scored 85) and Singapore (ranked 4, scored 85) are the best performing countries based on the CPI. In contrast, countries such as Somalia (ranked179, scored 12), South Sudan (rank 179, scored 12) and Syria (ranked 178, scored 14) are among the worst (Transparency International, 2020). In 2020, Barbados scored 64 with a ranking of 29 out of 180 countries. Barbados' ratings and scores on the CPI reflect the best in the region over the last decade.

Who dictates whether the CPI is a good corruption metric? According to Hawthorne (2012), Transparency International highlights a system of North-South historical divides that have been perpetuated for years. The systems in the North are used as a yardstick for assessing the systems in the South, despite the differences in location, politics, the economy and the various socio-historical influences, which should not be the case. The CPI, however, is what is used in the region to track countries' corruption standing. By examining the countries with the highest scores, it is possible to investigate the methods for achieving the same. Its methodology is as follows:

> 'The Corruption Perceptions Index is a composite index, a combination of different international surveys and assessments of corruption, collected by a variety of reputable institutions. The index draws on 13 surveys from independent institutions specialising in governance and business climate analysis covering expert assessments and views of businesspeople. None of these surveys were commissioned by Transparency International' (Transparency International, 2017).

Table 1. Barbados' TI's scores and rankings since 2010

Barbados CPI scores (out of 100)	2020	2019	2018	2017	2016	2014	2013	2012	2011	2010
	64	62	68	68	61	74	75	76	78	No Score
Barbados CPI rank-ings	2020 ranked 29/180	2019 ranked 30/180	2018 ranked 25/180	2017 ranked 25/180	2016 ranked 31/180	2014 ranked 17/180	2013 ranked 15/180	2012 ranked 15/180	2011 ranked 16/180	2010 No rank

Source: Transparency International website.

In 2020, the rankings/scores of some other Caribbean countries were as follows; Bahamas (ranked 30, scored 63), St Lucia (ranked 45, scored 56), Dominica (ranked 48, scored 55), Grenada (ranked 52, scored 53), Jamaica (ranked 69, scored 44) and Trinidad and Tobago (ranked 86, scored 40). The complete scores for Barbados are shown in Table 1.

It is arguable that the perception of Barbados' performance in the CPI is due to its stable economy, low crime rate enhanced by law enforcement and independent judicial system. The culture of law and order in post-colonial society is posited to be a result of the adherence shown to the laws of the country, which are strictly enforced by the police. Importantly, the country's social safety nets (low-cost health care, quality education, reduced taxes, etc.) are likely to serve as an incentive for most citizens to not run afoul of the law. The Barbados experience highlights that another 'likely possibility is a country's level of development, as richer countries might be able to 'afford' to spend more money on social services and redistribution of wealth while also addressing corruption' (World Bank, 2000). The preceding statement could explain why Barbados' anti-corruption framework has been successful over the years.

1.3 Socio-economic and political context

Barbados is the easternmost island of the Lesser Antilles in the West Indies. The capital and largest town is Bridgetown, which is also the main seaport (De Vere Phillips, 2021). As of 2019, the country recorded a population of 287,025 (World Bank Group, 2021). Most people – more than nine-tenths of the population – are of African descent (ibid.) (Figure 1) but all are described as 'Bajans'. The official language of the island is English. The Barbados' police to population ratio is 489 police per 100,000 people (The Gleaner, 2018). There are two major political parties: the Barbados Labour Party (BLP) and the Democratic Labour Party (DLP).

Most of the population is Christian (Figure 2). Anglicanism constitutes the largest percentage of the population with 23.9 per cent, Pentecostals are the second largest group (19.5 per cent) and the next largest groups are Seventh-day Adventists (5.9 per cent), followed by Methodists (4.2 per cent) (Barbados Integrated Government, 2021). There is significant religious diversity, however, with other smaller groups

Figure 1. Barbados ethnic composition

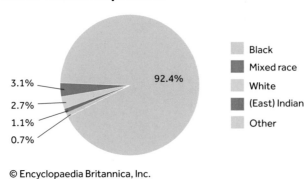

© Encyclopaedia Britannica, Inc.

including Moravians, Jehovah's Witnesses, Roman Catholics, Baha'i, Jews, Hindus and Muslims (De Vere Phillips, 2021).

The economy

Barbados has an open market economy, with services, manufacturing and agriculture being the most significant sectors. It receives remittances from Barbadians overseas and has a relatively high per capita income. Tourism is vital to the economy as the chief foreign exchange earner as well as a major employer. The gross domestic product (GDP) was US$5.209 billion as at 2019 (see Figure 3). Barbados had an overall ranking in 2020 of 128 out of 190 countries and scored 57.9 for ease of doing business, according to the World Bank (World Bank Group, 2020).

Education

Barbados' education system adheres closely to British norms. The nation enjoys an exceptionally high literacy rate of 99.6 percent. This success is attributable to the presence of a comprehensive government-funded primary and secondary school network. The Government places a high priority on education, allocating it a

Figure 2. Barbados religious affiliation

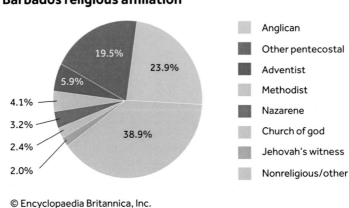

© Encyclopaedia Britannica, Inc.

Figure 3. Barbados' GDP for the past 10 years

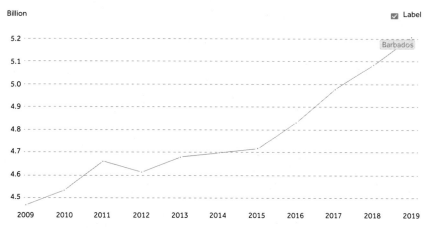

Source: World Bank Group, 2021.

significant portion of the budget. All education in public institutions is free (De Vere Phillips, 2021).

2. Methodology

A mixed methodology approach was taken to meet the requirements of this study, with the study period spanning from 1 March to 30 April 2021. The overall goal was to garner as much information on the systems, institutions and processes that bolstered the primary anti-corruption framework in Barbados. The study was, however, unsuccessful in scheduling interviews with members of the private sector, mainstream media, religious groups, academia and the parliamentary opposition as these groups did not respond to the request to be interviewed by the researcher. In total there was an approximately 37 per cent response rate and less than 20 per cent interview success.

2.1 Interviews

There was a total of 12 virtual/telephone interviews with an average time of 45 minutes per session. Interviewees included scholars and practitioners within the anti-corruption landscape in Barbados, as well as members from civil society, a youth group representative, a Senator, a Senior Lecturer at the Cave Hill Campus and representatives of international institutions/donor agencies.

Each participant was invited to participate in the study by email along with an introductory letter and, following their confirmation, an interview protocol. The Zoom meeting details were then provided. The interview structure included a brief introduction to the study and the researcher, along with a reminder of the interview protocol, followed by the interview questions and a wrap-up segment. The interviews explored the different factors that might have led to Barbados' successes in the anti-corruption landscape.

Based on the experiences of the participants, purposive, convenience and snowball sampling methods were used (Hays & Singh, 2012). These strategies are used in descriptive and exploratory studies and are suitable for studies such as this one. They allowed the researcher to collect data from stakeholders, creating a dialogue around the anti-corruption topic. Convenience and snowball sampling were especially necessary considering the pandemic and respondents' limited availability. The main challenge was recruiting participants, with less than 20 per cent interview success. No compensation was given in exchange for the participants' involvement in this study.

2.2 Survey instrument

The survey instrument was developed based on the findings from the initial interviews. The underlying themes of prevention, detection and public education were used to compile a total of 32 questions. (Appendix A). A total of four respondents completed the survey out of over fifty invitations.

2.3 Document analysis

A review was undertaken of the relevant laws, legislative agenda, reports, newspaper articles and other related documents on the topic of tackling corruption over the past 10 years. Thematic coding was used to analyse the information provided in the documents by identifying relevant document sources (articles/ books): assessing reliability and validity of sources: skimming documents for relevance to the research topic, reading the documents in a more fulsome manner: interpreting the documents (thematic analysis): and deriving main categories for thematic analysis (Bowen, 2009). The thematic analysis was an iterative process using a table to collate and compile similar themes, thus unearthing useful data for this study.

3. The legal and institutional framework

3.1 Legal framework

Most recently, the *Anti-Corruption and Anti-Terrorism Agency Act* was passed by the Senate on 26 March 2021. This law complements the *Prevention of Corruption Act (1929),* which was the only anti-corruption law for nearly 90 years. It should be noted that in 2012, the then Government passed the *Prevention of Corruption Act (2012-31)* but, though later assented to by the Governor General, the law was not proclaimed. There has also been the passage of the *Public Finance Management Act, 2019,* and amendments to existing laws to include the *Money Laundering and Financing of Terrorism (Amendment) (Prevention and Control) Act, 2019, Money Laundering and Financing of Terrorism (Prevention and Control) (Amendment) (No.2) Act, 2019,* and the *Anti-Terrorism (Amendment) Act, 2019.*

It is important to note that the Government, in passing the *Public Finance Management Act,* 2019, demonstrates the strengthening of fiscal responsibility and accountability. The introduction to the law states: 'Notwithstanding subsection (1)(b) and subsection (2), where loss, wastage, or improper use of monies of the Government occurs as a result of the decision of the Minister, the Minister is liable for the loss, wastage, or improper use of the monies of the Government'.

No anti-corruption law was passed in Barbados in 2020 due to the following occurrences described by *Barbados Today* (2020):

> 'Ten Government Senators who were present voted in favour of the bill. Two independent Senators abstained – Senators Toni Moore and Reverend John Rogers. Opposition Senators Caswell Franklyn and Crystal Drakes, along with two independent senators, Monique Taitt and Lindell Nurse, had earlier walked out of the Chamber. They raised strong objections to the return of Senator Lisa Cummins who had been advised to self-isolate by the Chief Medical Officer after she was among officials who welcomed Ghanaian nurses to the island. Nine of those nurses tested positive for the coronavirus. Senator Cummins tested negative for COVID-19 and was cleared to return to the Senate by the Chief Medical Officer'.

However, the *Remediation Agreements (Deferred Prosecutions) Act, 2020* was passed. It is akin to legislation passed in the UK that allows the Government to contract (do business) with a company against which allegations of corruption have been levelled.

The successful adoption and implementation of recommendations associated with AML/CFT measures by the Barbados regulatory framework are a culmination of years of hard work and dedication predating the present Government. It must be noted that Former Prime Minister of Barbados, Freundel Stuart in 2018 said that corruption is neither 'an invention or creation of the Democratic Labour Party', "...corruption was around long before the party, as is evident by the *Prevention of Corruption Act* which came into effect in 1929. He said corruption is an issue for the law and should not be used as a 'political football'(Loop Barbados News, 'Colleague' Innocent until proven guilty, August 12, 2018). Importantly from as far back as May 2010, the DPL had signalled the introduction of a Public Integrity Measure: "...Attorney General and Deputy Prime Minister Freundel Stuart commented on the Integrity Law being in its final stages of drafting...the new law would embrace civil servants and some officers of the private sector. Stuart said the public integrity measure, having public figures account for their assets', might be introduced soon very soon... He said that the public integrity bill ... 'was intended to be far-reaching' as the Government seeks to raise the level of public accountability for civil servants, lawmakers and certain sections of the private sector".(Nation News, Call to account, Tony Best, Posted May 30, 2010)

Importantly, it must be noted that there are other pieces of legislation that have not been passed and remain before the Parliament as Bills. These Bills are relevant for further influencing and defining the political will and the anti-corruption landscape in Barbados and are to be re-tabled in 2021: the Public Procurement Bill, 2018, Prevention of Corruption Bill, 2019 and Integrity in Public Life Bill, 2020. The Government has also indicated its intention to strengthen the anti-corruption framework by the passage of the Freedom of Information Bill and the Whistle-blowers Protection Bill.

3.2 Institutional framework

The Office of the Attorney General is the primary institution coordinating anti-corruption strategies. The constitutionally enshrined Office of the Director of Public Prosecutions (ODPP) is the sole prosecutorial authority and this, in conjunction with the Attorney General's chambers, the Royal Barbados Police Force (RBPF), the Auditor General's Office, the Anti-Money Laundering Authority (AMLA), the Financial Intelligence Unit (FIU) and the newly established Anti-Corruption and Anti-Terrorism Agency, forms the institutional framework for tackling corruption in Barbados (see Figure 4). The Government has made it a priority to strengthen the anti-corruption framework through its legal structure and a whole-of-community approach.

Office of the Attorney General

The Office of the Attorney General, Barbados, 'deals with constitutional affairs and judicial system of the country, civil and criminal law, prosecutions, and rehabilitation of offenders' (Government of Barbados, 2022). There are 16 departments within the Office, to include court administration, the Director of Public Prosecutions and the Financial Intelligence Unit (FIU). These departments help in the fight against corruption through their continued legal efforts, in conjunction with institutions such as Fulcrum, the Anti-Money Laundering Authority (AMLA) and the RBPF.

Office of the Department of Public Prosecutions (ODPP)

The Department of Public Prosecutions is the national prosecution service for the Island. It was established to prosecute cases instituted by the police. The police are responsible for the investigation of crime. Although the Department of Public Prosecutions works closely with the police, it is independent of them. Furthermore, the ODPP issues a Code for Crown Prosecutors as good practice, giving guidance

Figure 4. Barbados' primary anti-corruption institutions

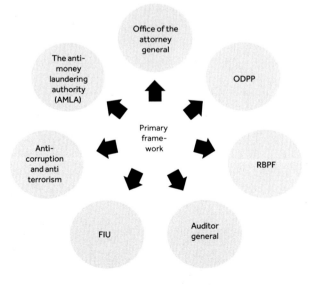

Figure 5. Primary anti-corruption legal framework in Barbados

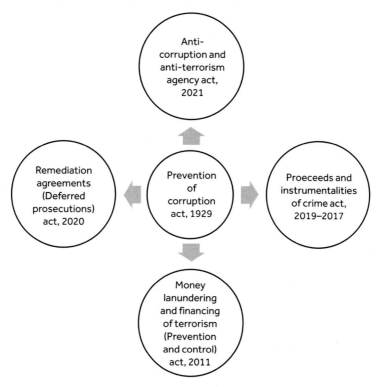

on the general principles to be applied when making decisions about prosecutions. Pursuant to the *Prevention of Corruption Act 1929* no prosecution under that Act shall be instituted except with the consent of the DPP, reiterating the fact that the ODPP serves as the sole authority to prosecute acts of corruption(Prevention of Corruption Act, Barbados).

Auditor-General's Office The Barbados Audit Office (2021) states that,

> 'The [...] Office was established in 1855 under the Act for Better Auditing and Inspecting of Public Accounts. The Office of the Auditor General exists to serve the Legislative Assembly and the people of Barbados. Under the Barbados Constitution the Auditor General is the Auditor of all government ministries, departments, funds and government-controlled entities. The Auditor General reports annually to the House of Assembly and his reports highlight issues requiring the attention of Parliament. It also contains recommendations that assist government organisations to improve their performance.'

The key role and contribution of the Audit Office to the fight against corruption is to hold administrators accountable for the administration and stewardship of public funds. The Auditor-General has independently initiated special examinations into the financial management of ministries, departments, statutory authorities and government-controlled entities, citing inefficiencies and ineffectiveness of the use of government resources.

Royal Barbados Police Force (RBPF)

The RBPF was founded in 1835, and its current Financial Crime Investigation Unit (FCIU) was created with the primary role to probe public corruption, fraud and terrorism financing. However, they lack the expertise and human resources to tackle public corruption and focus mainly on fraud and criminal investigations.

Anti Money Laundering Authority (AMLA)

AMLA was established by statute under the *Money Laundering and Financing of Terrorism (Prevention and Control) Act, 2011* to prevent money laundering and the financing of terrorism. Its key role is to monitor and supervise financial institutions in accordance with this Act. As it stands currently, the Director of the FIU is subject to the direction of the Authority.

Financial Intelligence Unit (FIU)

The FIU is responsible for the day-to-day work of AMLA. It is an administrative-type unit: a centralised, independent, administrative authority that receives and processes information from the financial sector and transmits disclosures to judicial or law enforcement authorities for prosecution. The FIU's role is strategic as it acts as a 'buffer' between the financial and the law enforcement communities (Financial Intelligence Unit of Barbados, 2021). FIU strives 'to be a centre of excellence in the receipt, analysis and the timely dissemination of financial intelligence within and outside of Barbados in order to effectively contribute to Barbados' reputation as a financially sound and stable jurisdiction for investment' (ibid.).

Barbados Public Accounts Committee

The Barbados Public Accounts Committee, established in 2003, has, over the past years served as an effective parliamentary committee that 'scrutinises the value for money – the economy, efficiency, and effectiveness – of public spending and generally holds the government and its civil servants to account for the delivery of public services' (Public Accounts Committee, 2008). The key role and duties of the Committee to the fight against corruption is 'to examine the audited financial statements …of all statutory corporations, entities owned or controlled by the Crown…' (Barbados Chapter 10A, Public Accounts Committee 2003-12, The Barbados Parliament)

Association of Certified Money Laundering Specialists (ACAMS)

ACAMS launched its Barbados chapter, one of 64 globally, in 2019. It serves as the Anti-Money Laundering (AML) hub in the Caribbean and seeks to foster the exchange of ideas and information amongst Caribbean professionals dedicated to the detection and prevention of money laundering and terrorist financing. (ACAMS TODAY, Introducing the ACAMS Barbados Chapter: The Caribbean Hub)

Its key role is to monitor anti-corruption strategies within the country and to provide best practices for anti-money laundering systems to the various institutions.

ACAMS' contribution to the fight against corruption is self evident as the 'largest international membership organisation dedicated to fighting financial crime' (ACAMS, 2021). The organisation boasts that,

> 'we are committed to enhancing the knowledge and skills of our members, which include financial crime detection and prevention of money laundering and terrorist financing, fostering exchange of ideas and information amongst Caribbean professionals from a wide range of financial institutions, regulatory bodies, law enforcement agencies and industry sectors.' (Ibid.)

Having a chapter in Barbados has had the effect of enhancing the Government's continued efforts to fight the impact of corruption, whilst strengthening the anti-corruption regime.

Fulcrum Chambers

The United Kingdom (UK)-based Fulcrum Chambers, a group of 'highly specialised legal advisory and consultancy business comprising barristers, solicitors, investigators and other high calibre professionals', has been engaged by the Government on a phased basis to investigate financial crimes and other forms of corruption (Madden, 2020). Fulcrum's presence is intended to not only investigate alleged corruption but also to bring those matters to the fore.

4. The Culture of Moral Conduct and Order

Barbados is historically an orderly society where citizens show a high level of discipline to rules and authority (Thame, 2014). Specifically, one interviewee stated that 'it's the culture, this is our way of life, to be honest, and kind, and to care for our fellow man'. Former Prime Minister, the Rt. Honourable Owen Arthur, PC stated that,

> 'our [Barbados'] material success has always been rooted in the determination of Barbadians of all walks to see the country succeed; to make the most of what we have, to make a sense of nationalism a real driving force in our development, and to draw psychic strength from attributes such as self-discipline, the virtues of industry, thrift, honesty, care of our inheritance, a feel for orderliness and a willingness to be our brother's keeper.' (1999, p. 4)

Similarly, the current Prime Minister, the Rt. Honourable Mia Mottley, QC, MP, leading up to the 2018 general elections, highlighted in the Barbados Labour Party's (BLP) manifesto 'Building the Best Barbados Together' that the BLP would, in the pursuit of good governance, weed out corruption;

> 'the Barbados Labour Party stands for strengthening the spiritual and cultural psyche of Barbadians in a way that enhances honesty and integrity, raises self-awareness, builds confidence and pride [and] fosters a sense of industry and responsibility, community and nationalism.' (Barbados Labour Party, 2018, p. 3)

Since 2018 the Government has made a concerted effort to bring a suite of legislation to the Parliament and to collaborate with and engage stakeholders on anti-corruption strategies. Whereas much more needs to be done, in a timely manner, its political will is acknowledged.

The Government has made several attempts to engage the private and civil sectors, media and international organisations. For example, during 2014 to 2016 the Inter-American Development Bank (IDB) has funded the modernization of the Barbados National Procurement System.

> 'The project was designed to support activities in four strategic areas: (i) creation of a central regulatory and normative body … to monitor and assess procurement activities in accordance with international best practices, as applicable, while taking into account developments within the Caribbean Single Market Economy (CSME) Government Procurement regime; (ii) more efficient management of the common goods and services procurement through the Central Purchasing Department, which will generate greater economy of scale; (iii) de-centralization of specialised goods and services procurement carried out by ministries and departments (i.e Barbados Drug Service, defence/security); and (iv) standardisation of various aspects of the procurement process carried out by all public entities, which will increase transparency, accountability and utilisation of the system. The project's strategic areas are reflected in four components that were to be implemented over a five-year period.' (IDB Project Completion Report, 2017)

The Integrity Group Barbados has participated in roundtable discussions, International Anti-Corruption Day celebrations and advocacy related to the anti-corruption agenda in Barbados.

The United Nations Office on Drugs and Crime (UNODC) conducted workshops towards implementation and ratification of the United Nations Convention Against Corruption (UNCAC). UNODC facilitated training in anti-corruption strategies in conjunction with the Office of the Attorney General (20 September 2017). Ms Bo Shakira Harris, Associate Programme Management Officer, states that UNODC offered support to Barbados in the following ways:

1. Reviewing the new Bill on Integrity in Public Life.

2. Conducting high-level meetings related to UNCAC ratification.

3. Guiding the design and drafting of a National Anti-Corruption Strategy.

4. Presenting a legislative analysis of the Bill on Integrity in Public Life in August 2018, with recommendations in line with the standards of the UNCAC.

5. Conducting high-level meetings and a workshop to support UNCAC ratification in September 2018 and delivering an inter-institutional workshop for the 'Design and Implementation of a National Anti-Corruption Strategy'.

6. Pursuing follow-up high-level meetings, particularly with the Attorney General and the Minister of Foreign Affairs, on the way forward.

7. Continuing to advocate for the ratification of the UNCAC and remaining ready to assist Barbados with technical assistance linked to the ratification of the Convention.

The European Union (EU) and the World Bank Group representatives shared that they currently have no policies or strategies in place to tackle anti-corruption in Barbados.

NGO's, Academia, the Bar Association and parts of the main and alternative media community have sensitised their membership and the public at large on issues related to anti-corruption best practices.

Barbadians have a strong sense of nationalism and high levels of social order, and the roles of the police and the education system have in a significant way defined their attributes of self-discipline, honesty, hard work and orderliness. They are reluctant to publicly discuss or share a viewpoint on the Government's handling of anti-corruption efforts or the perception of corruption. This approach does not mean ignoring the fact that a problem exists; rather, it is out of a sense of nationalism and pride that Barbadians disapprove of discussing matters that may be embarrassing, in public or with other people.

The efficiency and effectiveness of the RBPF coupled with the sanctions associated with the *Public Order Act* and the apprehension of citizens to be held in breach of the *Defamation Act* serve as deterrents to social disorder.

The Democratic Labour Party (DLP) has indicated its commitment to fight corruption. DLP's President Velda De Peiza stated that the party would have zero tolerance for corruption of any kind in high office: 'What we have always said from the beginning is that we eschew any shade of disrespect to our electoral system and abuse of power' (Mounsey, 2020). Furthermore, she called the Donville Inniss case[1], a cautionary tale for all politicians, persons in public life, and corporate entities. We all now need to learn the lesson of this bleak day and ensure that it never ever happens again' (Deane, 2020). Donville Innis "a former member of Barbados Parliament Sentenced to 24 months in Prison for Money Laundering Scheme; laundered bribe payments from a Barbados based insurance company through banks on Long Island… engaged in bribery and money laundering scheme to line his own pockets at the expense of the people of Barbados" (Department of Justice, U.S. Attorneys Office, Eastern District of New York, April 2021)

The selection of the Office of Chief Justice and Puisne Judges is now subject to a process including the advertisement of vacancies and inviting applications.

5. Discussion

To meet the demands of this research, various data collection methods were used such as conducting interviews, desk reviews and distributing a survey instrument. The results of the survey and interviews were underwhelming as the response rate was low. This could suggest that there is a culture of silence in Barbados. On the other hand, it could also suggest that the citizens are satisfied with the efforts made by the Government to combat corruption issues and therefore do not see the need to speak on the matter. However, it is arguably the former, as most Barbadians display a deep sense of nationalism, steeped in pride, and to publicly discuss issues of corruption facing the country could conceivably have the effect of embarrassing their national pride.

Barbados is a society that instils the values of order and peace from a tender age (Thame, 2014). These values translate into an orderly society where most youth and adults are committed to respecting law enforcement authorities and more so the rule of law, presumably strongly settled in the belief system that good behaviour is rewarded and bad behaviour is not. Several of the participants shared the importance of the Barbadian culture in shaping the moral fabric of the society.

It may be argued that there is a correlation between a law-abiding society and consistently high scores on the CPI ranking. For example, the maintenance of law and order in other countries such as Finland, Singapore and Sweden that rank high on the CPI is acknowledged. Further, Barbados has a stable economy, a high police-to-citizen ratio and an efficient policing system and there are not many reported cases of corruption. The laws also bolster the transparency of public funds' management and reporting systems. It could therefore be strongly argued that the reason for these successes is directly related to the maintenance of law and order, self-discipline, honesty and fiscal discipline.

The fact that corruption is not perceived to be as high in Barbados as in other countries in the region can be attributed to a concerted effort being made to address the scourge over the past 10 years. But notice must be taken of the remarkable fact that the country does not have in place the anti-corruption governance and accountability framework that exists in some of its counterparts in the Eastern Caribbean or Jamaica. The Government must be credited, but the single most critical factor (highlighted above) is the Barbadians' strong sense of nationalism, the high levels of social order and the roles of the police and the education system in defining the attributes of self-discipline, honesty and orderliness.

Also, importantly, Barbados has actively engaged international organisations such as UNODC and the IDB and, through social partnerships with its citizenry, has been able to 'bridge the gap' in the absence of a single anti-corruption network. In addition, the Government has sought the assistance of other international groups such as Fulcrum and continues to use international best practices for tackling corruption. Local organisations including civil society (the Integrity Group Barbados), the Bar Association and other stakeholders have also been invited within the last three years to engage with the Government through submissions on critical pieces of legislation touching and concerning the anti-corruption regime. This whole-of-community approach contributes significantly to the country's successes in advancing anti-corruption strategies.

At the same time, the Government ought to fast track the implementation of a single anti-corruption regime. Of greater importance, countries within the region should consider implementing more robust public education strategies within the anti-corruption framework through a whole-of-community approach where multiple stakeholders are engaged, especially the youth. The main thrust of the public education strategy must be to reinforce the attributes of self-discipline, honesty and the maintenance of law and order as are evident in Barbados.

 Promulgation of the *Remediation Agreements (Deferred Prosecution) Act 2020* and its stated objects 'to provide for a prosecutor, in relation to certain offences, to enter into an agreement to defer prosecution of an alleged offender and impose certain obligations on the offender, where such an agreement would be in the interest of justice' must be acknowledged as an international best practice and a tool that should be adopted by countries in the region in fighting corruption. The law is progressive and, if 'buy in' occurs, it may serve to benefit the offender, the criminal justice system and the anti-corruption state apparatus. This prevention tool is a strategic one for the anti-corruption fight and is strongly recommended for countries in the region.

6. Challenges, Lessons and Recommendations

6.1 Challenges

Attorney General and Minister of Legal Affairs, Hon. Dale Marshall, QC, MP, recently told the House of Assembly that,

> 'We know that issues of corruption require an eye to detail, and it also requires in many instances the application of skill sets that are not readily available very often in Barbados. We believe that in order to be able to be (sic) adequately deal with the issue of corruption we need to move beyond the operation of the RBPF and establish a dedicated agency that goes to work every single day to investigate corruption and terrorism issues ... Part of the reason why we've been unable to make any strides on that particular index is because all that we have had is an RBPF struggling to deal with everything that it has to struggle to deal with and with a 1929 piece of legislation. I mean it is a wonder we were anywhere at all.' (Bennett, 2021)

The RBPF lacks the institutional capacity to tackle corruption. Its Financial Crime Investigation Unit (FCIU), created to probe public corruption, fraud and terrorism financing, lacks expertise and human resources. RBPF records indicate five corruption-related offences being disposed of in 2017 and six in 2019, totalling eleven matters dealt with between 2016 and 2020. No statistics were received for the period 2010 to 2016. The RBPF will not investigate any matter unless a formal report is made to them by a complainant.

There are no campaign financing laws or modern regulations governing spending by candidates during an election campaign.

The Attorney General and Minister of Legal Affairs, with reference to the Donville Inniss case, stated,

> 'it is significant that the conviction came about because individuals who had knowledge of the events were prepared to speak out and to give evidence about wrongdoing.' (Nation News, 2020)

The Barbados parliamentary caucus has encountered issues with the timely passing of legislation. Directly related to this is the need for public announcements in the mainstream and social media affording advance notice to all stakeholders of impending legislative changes. Information about changes to legislation is not always communicated to the public and stakeholders promptly.

The Government is also experiencing a data deficit gap, which draws attention to the areas for improvement in the collection and storage of data and making them available to be utilised as a measuring tool to assess the anti-corruption framework.

6.2 Lessons

The key lessons that can be drawn from the Barbados case are related to the institutional framework, legal system and culture of the people.

1. The Government has, over the past years, implemented several strategies that seek to bolster the anti-corruption institutional framework. The current efforts to expand the anti-corruption and anti-terrorism legal framework is grounded in years of hard work, trial and error and a whole-of-community approach that includes the public and private sectors and institutions. Through training, consultancy and engagement, the Government has 'bridged the gap' in the absence of a single anti-corruption regime. Its efforts are comparable to if not surpassing the governance and accountability systems in the Eastern Caribbean islands or the single anti-corruption model in Jamaica. Other countries in the Commonwealth can benefit from the inclusive approach to problem solving that Barbados has instituted in the fight against corruption.

2. The legal framework in Barbados is a robust one, with the legislative agenda playing a major role in the creation and building of the anti-corruption landscape. Countries within the Commonwealth should make a concerted effort to implement anti-corruption strategies and promulgate laws, and the role of the Legal Reform Commissions should be energised. The laws should be implemented with purpose and with a vision of achieving benchmarks in a stated period. However, each country must be cognizant of the powerful message of UNODC that there is no single model of reform; instead, leadership in each country must determine priorities and the appropriate sequencing of steps towards implementation (UNCAC, 2007).

3. Countries within the Commonwealth must make it a priority to instil values of discipline, law and order from a tender age. These values should be inculcated through the school system, religious institutions and the family structure. In almost all the interviews, the participants shared that the Barbadian culture was symbolic of each citizen subjecting himself or herself to the principles of law and order.

4. Activist groups play a vital role in the fight against the impact of corruption in Barbados. The Integrity Group Barbados, led by Attorney-at-law Alicia Archer, is one such group that uses its platform to raise awareness on the impact of

corruption. Additionally, the Group actively engages with the Government to bring matters of corruption and plausible solutions to the fore.

6.3 Recommendations

1. An anti-corruption public education programme should be conceptualised and implemented. The engagement of stakeholders began in earnest in 2018; however, a national programme could be created and extended to the youth, service groups and target areas. Even though they have 'bridged the gap' in the absence of a national programme, the formalisation of this best practice ought to be considered.

2. The Barbados parliamentary caucus must make it a matter of urgency and a priority to debate and pass legislation in a timely manner. More importantly, public announcements in mainstream media and social media affording advance notice to all stakeholders of impending legislative changes would be welcomed. It would further signal that the passage of anti-corruption-related legislation (for example, the Freedom of Information Act and Whistle-blowing Act) is prioritised, as in the case of legislation related to Anti-Money Laundering (AML)/CFT), counter-terrorism and the financing of illicit and illegal activities.

3. The Government must urgently fast track closing the data deficit gap and prioritise the collection, storage and availability of data that could be utilised and included as a part of a measuring tool to assess the anti-corruption framework.

4. Barbados ought to consider the implementation of a single anti-corruption regime, allowing international agencies and donors to interface directly and facilitating regular and periodic technical support and training in keeping with emerging and existing international best practices. This is a work-in-progress in Barbados, given the many attempts by the Government to improve upon their anti-corruption and anti-terrorism efforts.

5. Some international agencies and donors have had no recent anti-corruption programmes in Barbados. It would be useful upon the implementation of a single anti-corruption institution to engage these in providing technical support in keeping with international best practices and emerging trends.

Note

1 The Donville Inniss case refers to the 16 January 2020 conviction of a former Barbados Minister of Industry, International Business Commerce and Small Business Development. Inniss was convicted for two counts of money laundering and one count of conspiracy to commit money laundering in the Eastern District Federal Court in New York.

Bibliography

ACAMS TODAY, Introducing the ACAMS Barbados Chapter, the Caribbean Hub, December 22, 2020. https://www.acamstoday.org

AMLA (Anti-Money Laundering Authority) (2019) *Annual Reports 2013–2018*. Bridgetown: Financial Intelligence Unit. https://barbadosfiu.gov.bb/wp-content/

uploads/2019/12/FIU-Annual-Report-2013-2018.pdf,   Barbados   Integrated Government

Arthur, O (1999) 'The Sociology of Our Development'. Address by the Rt. Hon. Owen Arthur, PM on the occasion of the Launching of the Committee for National Reconciliation on July 28th 1999. Report of the Committee for National Reconciliation, A Shared Vision For the 21st Century, Volume 2, December 2000. https://docstore.ohchr.org

Barbados Audit Office (2021) 'Our Mission'. http://barbadosauditoffice. adaangdbarbados.net

Barrow-Gille, C (2011) 'Democracy at Work: A Comparative Study of the Caribbean State'. *The Round Table* 100(414): 285–302.

Barbados Today (2020) 'We're Down, but Not Out Over the Integrity Bill'. Editorial, 6 August. https://barbadostoday.bb

Barbados Underground (2016) 'Public Accounts Committee and Auditor General Must Recommit to Holding Public Officers Accountable'. https:// barbadosunderground.net

Bennett, R (2021) 'New Anti-Corruption, Counter-Terrorism Agency "Necessary" – AG'. *Barbados Today*, 10 March. https://barbadostoday.bb/2021/03/10/ new-anti-corruption-counter-terrorism-agency-necessary-ag/

Best, T (2020) 'Call to Account'. *NationNews*. www.nationnews.com

Bowen, GA (2009) 'Document Analysis as a Qualitative Research Method'. *Qualitative Research Journal* 9(2), 27–40.

Deane, S (2020) 'DLP Says Inniss' Guilty Verdict Is a Sad Day for Barbados'. *Barbados Today*, 16 January. https://barbadostoday.bb/2020/01/16/dlp-says-inniss-guilty -verdict-is-a-sad-day-for-barbados/

De Vere Phillips, A (2021) 'Barbados'. *Encyclopedia Britannica*. https://www. britannica.com/place/Barbados

Financial Intelligence Unit of Barbados (2021) 'About Us'. https://barbadosfiu.gov.bb/ about-us/

Government of Barbados (2022). 'Office of the Attorney General (AG)'. https://www. gov.bb/Ministries/attorney-general

Hawthorne, OE (2015) *Do International Corruption Metrics Matter? The Impact of Transparency International's Corruption Perception Index*. Lanham, MD: Lexington Books. https://digitalcommons.odu.edu

Hays, DG and AA Singh (2012) *Qualitative Inquiry in Clinical and Educational Settings*. New York: The Guilford Press.

Hinds, K (2019) *Civil Society Organisations, Governance, and the Caribbean Community*. Basingstoke, UK: Palgrave Macmillan.

Inter-American Development Bank Project Completion Report: Investment Loan. *Project Name:* Modernization of The Barbados National Procurement System. Office of Evaluation and Oversight, Approach Paper, Barbados 2014-2018. https://publications/iadb.org

Loop Barbados News April 22, 2019 AG:Barbados working to comply with FATF standards

Madden, M (2020) 'Corrupt Barbados Officials Will 'Face the Court'. *Barbados Today*, 15 January. https://barbadostoday.bb/2020/01/15/corrupt-barbados-officials -will-face-the-court/

Mounsey, C (2020) 'US Trial "Could Not Hold up in Our Court" – DLP'. *Barbados Today*, 15 January. https://barbadostoday.bb/2020/01/15/us-trial-could-not -hold-up-in-our-court-dlp/

Nation News (2020) '*AG: People Were Prepared to Talk*'. 17 January. https://www. nationnews.com/2020/01/17/ag-people-were-prepared-to-talk/

ODPP (Office of the Director of Public Prosecutions) (2014) 'The Code for Public Prosecutors: Barbados'. Eastern Caribbean Law. http://www. gisbarbados.gov.bb

Schultz, J (2007) 'The United Nations Convention Against Corruption: A Primer for Development Practitioners'. Anti-Corruption Resource Centre U4 Brief no. 3. https://www.cmi.no

Smith, C (2018) 'Stuart: "Colleague' Innocent Until Proven Guilty"'. Loop News, 12 August. https://barbados.loopnews.com

Smith, KB and CW Larimer (2018) *The Public Policy Theory Primer*. 3rd edition. New York and London: Routledge.

Thame, M (2014) 'Disciplining the Nation: Considering the Privileging of Order over Freedom in Postcolonial Jamaica and Barbados'. *Social and Economic Studies* 63(2), 1–29.

The Gleaner (2018) 'Divest Police Authority to Private Security Firms'. Editorial, 29 January. https://jamaica-gleaner.com/article/commentary/20180130/editorial-divest-police-authority-private-security-firms

Transparency International, 27 January 2017

Transparency International (2020) *Corruption Perceptions Index 2020: Barbados*. https://www.transparency.org/en/cpi/2020/index/brb

U.S. Department of Justice, US Attorneys Office, Eastern District of New York, Press Release, Tuesday April 27, 2021. https://www.justice.gov

Weible, C and PA Sabatier (eds.) (2018) *Theories of the Policy Process*. 4th edition. New York: Routledge. https://www.vitalsource.com

World Bank Group (2020) *Doing Business 2020: Comparing Business Regulations in 190 Economies*. Washington, DC: World Bank. https://www.doingbusiness.org/en/doingbusiness

World Bank Group (2021) 'GDP (Current US$): Barbados'. https://data. worldbank.org/indicator/NY.GDP.MKTP.CD?end=2019&locations=BB&start=2009&view=chart

Appendix

Appendix. Research response success

Sector/group	Total	Number of attempts	Feed-back received	Number of interviews	Follow-up call/email
Public	10	20+	4	2	✓
Private	8	20+	2	2	✓
Parliamentarian/ independent Senators	11	20+	2	1	✓
Religious	6	15+	1	0	✓
Academia	7	15+	3	1	✓
Civil	6	10+	3	2	✓
Youth	4	10+	1	1	✓
Media	3	10+	1	0	✓
International organisation/do nor	8	15+	6	3	✓
Total	63	135+	23	12	**Success rate interviews <20% Responses ~37%**

Chapter 4

Dominica

Julian Johnson

Abstract

Dominica has had a long tradition of integrity and professionalism in its public service due mainly to a supportive legal framework and careful selection and training of its public servants. Very few incidents of corruption have occurred over the past 60 years. Like most other Eastern Caribbean countries, Dominica signed on to the United Nations Convention Against Corruption, the Inter-American Convention Against Corruption, the Convention on Extradition and the Convention on Mutual Assistance in Criminal Matters. The Government has also strengthened provisions for accountability and transparency in its legislation and institutions for audit, finance administration and the prevention of money laundering. It has recently enacted legislation for public procurement and contract administration and for integrity in public office. The major institutions engaged in corruption prevention have reached out to the public to gain their support in carrying out their functions as oversight and enforcement bodies. Recent experience has shown that legislation and institutional frameworks must be regularly reviewed and strengthened to allow for enhanced autonomy for and parliamentary oversight of oversight bodies. In addition, there should be vigorous public education and engagement on the deleterious effects of corruption in societies. Recommendations have been made for strengthening the composition of the Integrity Commission, timely tabling of the reports of oversight bodies in Parliament, sensitization of parliamentarians concerning their role at the apex of oversight institutions, funding of political parties and political campaigns, enhancing the independence of the Integrity Commission in staff recruitment and control and triennial reviews of the operation and effectiveness of oversight bodies.

1. Overview

Dominica is a small country in the Eastern Caribbean with a population estimated at 72,000 and gross domestic product (GDP) per capita of US$8,000 (World Bank, 2020). Once dependent on banana exports, the economy has shifted to tourism and financial services, an adjustment that has left the rural population especially vulnerable with respect to income distribution and investment financing. Dominica's public debt stands at about 78 per cent of GDP (Global Finance, 2019).

The Government is currently the leading sector in the economy. With GDP of US$0.6 billion, its share of expenditure is estimated at 55.6 per cent and of consumption expenditure (including employee compensation) at 21.3 per cent over the past three years (Miller et al., 2021). Government's share of the economy makes its framework for upholding integrity and combatting corruption especially critical for sustained and robust growth and development and for the equitable distribution of income and other benefits.

Historically, Dominica has had a long tradition of ethical conduct and professionalism among its civil servants due in part to regular and effective training of its senior managers, which has given them not only technical and professional skills but also a clear understanding of and confidence in their roles in the business of government and their authority under the Constitution and enabling statutes.

In general, a supportive legal framework has enabled the civil service to maintain a high degree of transparency and accountability in transacting government business and reporting directly to Parliament. Legislative reform measures to enhance accountability and transparency and limit opportunities for corruption in both the public and private sectors were introduced over the past two decades. Significantly, integrity in public office legislation brought within its ambit a classification of 'persons in public life', which includes the Cabinet, MPs and non-elected public officials who were not previously directly covered by the regulatory statutes.

Reform measures were also taken to establish and strengthen oversight institutions, including a new Central Procurement Board to ensure transparency and fairness in procurement contracts for goods, services and works; a financial services unit to oversee the operations of financial institutions; and an Integrity Commission to, inter alia, inquire into allegations of bribery and acts of corruption. As regards the operations of central Government, major reforms were carried out to systems and procedures to strengthen real-time integrated accounting and auditing so as to streamline and secure government financial transactions and produce timely and accurate reports and for real-time internal audit purposes.

Like most other Eastern Caribbean countries, Dominica is signatory to the United Nations Convention Against Corruption (UNCAC) and the Inter-American Convention Against Corruption (IACAC). It is also party to the Convention on Extradition and the Convention on Mutual Assistance in Criminal Matters.

Dominica's ranking on Transparency International's Corruption Perception Index (CPI) has shown varying results coming from a low point at 45.00 prior to 2006, to a high point at 59.00 in 2016 and, since then, to 55.00 by 2020 (see Table 1).

Dominica's Economic Freedom score (Heritage Foundation and Wall Street Journal), a measure of its performance in relation to regulatory efficiency, open markets, government size and the rule of law (judicial effectiveness, government integrity and property rights) also showed a corresponding decline mainly attributed to expanded

Table 1. Dominica's CPI

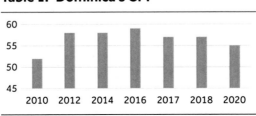

Table 2. Dominica's Economic Freedom score

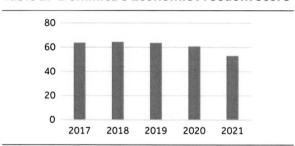

budget deficits and increased borrowing following the devastating effect of major disasters in 2015 and 2017 (see Table 2).

In its National Resilience Development Strategy 2030, the Government said that it 'fully committed to some basic principles for orderly national progress', inter alia, political stability, rule of law, equity and social order, responsiveness, effectiveness, transparency and accountability and macro-economic stability (Government of the Commonwealth of Dominica, 2015).

This research and study are to evaluate how these measures have impacted on the prevention of corruption in the Commonwealth of Dominica, challenges encountered in the process and lessons learnt from those experiences and to make recommendations for strengthening the legal and institutional framework as well as the socio-political environment for dealing with challenges in the future.

2. Methodology

The overall objective was to identify factors that have contributed to success in combatting corruption as well as the strategies employed by various oversight institutions engaged in anti-corruption activities, the challenges faced by them and the lessons learned from their collective experience. Accordingly, the following methodology was employed:

- Review of existing literature on efforts made to combat corruption, including the Hansard of the House of Assembly reporting on debates on legislation pertinent to anti-corruption legislation, information booklets and operational guidelines of the Integrity Commission, annual reports of the Integrity Commission, the Financial Intelligence Unit (FIU) and of the Director of Audit and assessment reports by the Conference of State Parties to UNCAC and the Organization of American States (OAS).

- Review of existing legislation governing the operations of oversight bodies, including related internal policies and procedures.

- Identification of organizations and institutions engaged in anti-corruption activities, the strategies they employed and their impact on the anti-corruption programme.

- Interviews with key stakeholders, including civil society, private sector representatives, officials of political parties and public officials, to gather information on their perception of the role and impact of oversight bodies.

- Research of newspaper and other media reports, commentaries and editorials related to anti-corruption efforts.

- Analysis of data on Dominica's rating on the CPI and the Index of Economic Freedom and identifying factors contributing to its performance.

3. Socio-Political Context

Dominica obtained independence in 1978 as a democratic republic founded on the principles of fundamental rights and freedoms. Its Parliament is unicameral with 21 members elected on a first past-the-post system and nine senators (five appointed by the prime minister and four by the leader of the opposition). Transitioning from a legislature dominated by planters and merchants, the island attained universal adult suffrage in 1951. The first political party emerged in 1955 from the conflict between an oligarchic administration and an increasingly strident workers' and peasants' movement. Three important social reforms shifted the balance of power from the former to the latter: the redistribution of lands formerly held by mostly absentee landlords, the formation of trade unions and the introduction of credit unions, all of which effectively re-distributed economic resources and social privilege.

The current elections statute is based on a multi-party system that allows fierce but orderly competition for voter support. While the election laws generally provide a level playing field for competing parties, there have emerged in recent times critical inequalities of resources that may be applied to election campaigns and that engender unequal or uneven advantages among competing parties. This situation has brought about several legal challenges as to the validity and fairness of election results, and calls have been made for a just and equitable code for election financing.

In addition to its ordinary law-making functions, Parliament has a crucial role as an oversight body through:

1. The general body's power to debate and question any matter on the order paper; and

2. The Public Accounts Committee's power to examine the accounts of Government together with the report of the Director of Audit.

However, delays in the submission of government accounts and the report of the Director of Audit have been major constraints in the functioning of the Public Accounts Committee. In this situation, the burden of oversight and corruption prevention falls on the oversight institutions that were recently established.

4. Genesis of the Anti-Corruption Regime

Even before independence, a framework for accounting for and reporting on the business of government, though restricted to public officers, served to encourage transparency and accountability in government transactions. The principal statutes for doing so included a *Finance and Audit Ordinance (1965)* that provided for the management of the public funds of the colony, the appropriation and issue of sums therefrom, the audit of public accounts and for other incidental or related matters including penalties for improper use of government funds and for loss or destruction of government property. This Ordinance was supported by updated financial regulations (1976) and by stores regulations (1980) for the custody, use and accounting for government monies and property. Neither the ordinance nor the regulations gave much attention to the important issue of public procurement. A *Money Laundering Act* for the prevention of money laundering and related matters was passed in 2000.

Major legal and institutional reforms to strengthen provisions for transparency and accountability after two decades of the workings of the ministerial system brought about independent audit legislation, an enhanced *Finance (Administration) Act 1994*, and a comprehensive *Public Procurement and Contract Administration Act 2012.*

General (administrative) orders establishing a code for the conduct of civil servants and for equity in matters related to appointments, compensation and discipline were replaced by the *Public Service Act 1991,* which provided for the establishment of the public service and the maintenance of its efficiency and for ensuring that advancement in the public service is based on the constitutional principle of the recognition of merit, ability and integrity.

During the same period, significant changes were made in the organization and computerization of transaction-sensitive agencies such as the Customs, Inland Revenue and the Accountant General's Office that effectively facilitated real-time accounting and reporting, inter-agency linkages and enhanced reporting systems that considerably improved management and audit capabilities.

The advances made in the legal and institutional framework post-independence coupled with careful selection and training of public service senior managers helped to maintain high ethical standards and levels of transparency and accountability that engendered public confidence and trust.

5. Constitutional, Legislative and Institutional Framework

5.1 Constitutional and legislative framework

Dominica's Independence Constitution (1978) and the Supreme Court Order established several autonomous oversight institutions and offices characteristic of the Westminster model of parliamentary democracy, with features that include an executive collectively responsible to Parliament, a non-partisan public service and police service appointed by independent Service Commissions, an independent judiciary, a Director of Public Prosecutions and a Parliamentary Commissioner (Ombudsman).

The Constitution mandates Parliament to both oversee and hold the Government to account. An audit institution, regulatory boards and anti-corruption agencies are required to report to Parliament annually. This is a means of both ensuring their independence from government, expressed in the formula and learning that 'in the exercise of their functions, they shall not be subject to the direction or control of any other person or authority' (See sections 72(6), 83(7) and 84(12) of the Commonwealth of Dominica Constitution Order 1978), and reinforcing Parliament's position at the apex of oversight institutions.

Under section 60 of the Constitution, the collective responsibility and accountability of the Cabinet and the individual ministers to Parliament have been made the central principle of Dominica's parliamentary democracy. This principle is enforced under the Standing Orders of the House of Assembly by means of questions, motions (including censor motions) and debates.

Under the *Audit Act 1994* and *Finance (Administration) Act 1994*, the financial administration of the State is further safeguarded by entrusting the management of and accounting for public funds to 'accounting officers' who are directly answerable to Parliament for all monies received and spent by government ministries and departments. The Accountant General and the Financial Secretary are empowered to exercise further scrutiny and tender advice on keeping departmental expenditures within limits and procedures set by Parliament through its statutes and votes procedures.

In compliance with international good practice and binding treaties, during the period 1994–2014, Parliament strengthened laws and established additional institutions for accountability, transparency and good governance to address international and domestic concerns of corruption.

Foremost among the body of anti-corruption legislation are:

1. The *Money Laundering Prevention Act 2011*, which – in response to international concern about illicit drug trafficking and the financing of terrorism – sought to hold accountable any person who aids, abets, counsels or procures the commission of or attempts or conspires to commit the offence of money laundering and to impose penalties therefor.

2. The *Extradition Act 1981*, as amended, to deal with fugitives from the criminal law in other states resident in Dominica, to adopt the principles formulated by the law ministers of the Commonwealth in their London conference of 1966 and to accord with international practice regarding the return of fugitives.

3. The *Mutual Assistance in Criminal Matters Act 1994* to make provision with respect to the scheme relating to mutual assistance in criminal matters within the Commonwealth and other countries.

4. The *Proceeds of Crime Act 1993*, as amended, for the forfeiture or confiscation of the proceeds of certain scheduled offences including money laundering, controlled drug trafficking and the financing of terrorism.

5. The *Public Procurement and Contract Administration Act 2012*, which came into force in January 2015 and applies to every ministry and non-ministerial department of the Government, local authorities and statutory bodies. It requires those institutions to ensure that their procurement activities and decisions are based on the principles of fairness and equitable treatment, competition,

economy, value for money, transparency and accountability, demand aggregation and foster and encourage broad participation in the procurement proceedings by persons in Dominica. If there is conflict between this Act in matters relating to public procurement and disposal, the Act shall prevail.

6. The *Finance Intelligence Unit Act 2011* empowers the FIU to receive, request, investigate and disseminate information concerning suspected proceeds of crime and suspicious transactions and information relating to the property of terrorist groups and terrorist financing under the *Money Laundering (Prevention) Act* or the *Suppression of the Financing of Terrorism Act*.

7. The *Financial Services Unit Act 2009* was enacted to deter financial crimes and applies to financial institutions including credit unions, development banks, exempt insurance companies, international business companies, internet gaming companies, offshore banks, insurance companies and money transfer companies.

8. The *Automatic Exchange of Financial Account Information (Common Reporting Standard) Act 2019* was enacted to provide for the implementation of Dominica's obligations arising under the Organisation for Economic Co-operation and Development (OECD) Convention of Mutual Administrative Assistance in Tax Matters, which was signed by the Government in April 2019 and is incorporated in the First Schedule to the Act. The taxes covered include those on income or profits, on capital gains and on wealth.

9. The *Integrity in Public Office Act 2003* was enacted in April 2003 but not brought into force until September 2008. This Act provides for the establishment of an Integrity Commission for the purpose of receiving declarations on the financial affairs of persons holding specific offices or positions and for the purpose of establishing probity, integrity and accountability in public life.

These legislative reforms, though deficient in some areas, helped to serve as a bulwark against external criminal activities and as a powerful deterrent against acts of corruption internally.

Dominica is a party to the Inter-American Convention Against Corruption (IACC), signed by all 34 members of the OAS in 2004. This declared the intention to set up mechanisms to prevent corruption including laws that provide provisions to establish bodies capable of doing so. In keeping with its obligations under the IACC, and the report of the expert group on good governance and the elimination of corruption in economic management established by the Commonwealth Heads of Governments Meeting at Edinburgh in 1997, Dominica reformed its legal framework to strengthen its capacity to prevent corruption.

Dominica is also a party to the United Nations Convention against Corruption (UNCAC), which entered into force in December 2005 and is a legally binding universal anti-corruption instrument. It covers different forms of corruption, such as bribery, abuse of functions and trading in influence, and it provides for prevention measures, criminalization and law enforcement, international cooperation, asset recovery, technical assistance and information exchange.

The United Nations Commission Against Corruption Implementation Review Group 2015 report on Dominica drew attention to some deficiencies that should be urgently addressed, among them the need for statutory definition for active bribery and a broader definition of passive bribery in the private sector (Conference of the State Parties to the United Nations Conference against Corruption, 2015). It also pointed out that 'legislation that specifically addresses embezzlement in the public or private sector' has not been enacted although a *Theft Act* does this in general terms (ibid., p. 3). Additionally, it observed that there are no regulations against abuse of functions. The report also noted the absence of legislation for the protection of witness, experts, victims and whistle-blowers, although provision has been made for witness protection.

5.2. Institutional framework

The following are the most important anti-corruption institutions.

Office of the Director of Audit

The Office of the Director of Audit is established under section 89 of the Constitution as an independent department of government reporting through the minister responsible for finance to Parliament with responsibility to examine the government accounts, report on them annually to Parliament and assist the Public Accounts Committee in its review of the accounts. As a member of the Caribbean Association of Supreme Audit Institutions (CAROSAI), it interacts with other Commonwealth audit institutions and shares best practice standards with them.

Integrity Commission

The Integrity Commission was established under the *Integrity in Public Office Act 2003*, as amended by the *Integrity in Public Office (Amendment) Act 2015*, to maintain probity, integrity and accountability in public life. The Commission consists of three members, two appointed on the advice of the Prime Minister and one on the advice of the Leader of the Opposition, with a quorum of two members present at any meeting. It is an independent body reporting through the minister responsible for legal affairs to Parliament. The Commission operates with limited power to receive and examine annual financial declarations and violations of the Code of Conduct prescribed for persons in public life, to refer to the police cases that require investigative action and to submit matters for criminal prosecution to the DPP. The Commission's staff are recruited from the public service and are appointed by the Public Service Commission.

The Commission is authorised to inquire into allegations of bribery or act of corruption, to receive and investigate complaints regarding non-compliance with any of its provisions and to make enquiries to verify or determine the accuracy of declarations filed with it. The Act criminalised the possession of unaccounted property or pecuniary resource disproportionate to legitimate sources of income, and the Commission is empowered to conduct inquiries into a declarant's source of income on suspicion of such unaccounted possession. It is instructed to make an annual report to the Minister for Legal Affairs, who is required to table it in the House of Assembly not later than three months after receipt.

Public Accounts Committee (PAC)

In matters of financial administration, the select committee of Parliament known as the PAC, chaired by the Leader of the Opposition, has the duty to examine the accounts of the Government together with the report of the Director of Audit on such accounts. Through hearings, in private, based on the Director of Audit's report, it holds accounting officers and other officers who are responsible for financial control to account. The PAC, in this watchdog role, is assisted and advised by the Director of Audit. Under section 83 of the Constitution, the Director of Audit is required to audit and report on the public accounts of the country and the accounts of all officers and authorities of the Government, the law courts and the accounts of every commission established by the Constitution and submit every such report to the Minister of Finance for laying in the House of Assembly no later than seven days after the House first meets after the Minister has received the report.

Financial Intelligence Unit

The *Financial Intelligence Unit Act 2011* established the FIU with powers to investigate financial crimes and, in particular, money laundering with responsibility to receive, request, analyse, investigate and disseminate information concerning suspicious transactions and to detect and pursue the proceeds of crime as to prevent money laundering and terrorist financing and other financial crimes. The FIU reports to Parliament annually through the minister responsible for legal affairs. The Director, who is the chief executive officer and advisor to the minister, heads the FIU, which is staffed by persons trained in the techniques of investigating financial crimes.

Financial Services Unit

The objective of the Unit is to facilitate public confidence in the financial system and facilitate the deterrence of financial crimes, ensure periodic evaluation of the legislative and regulatory framework, supervise financial services licences and promote best practices by maintaining contact and forging relations with foreign regulatory authorities and international associations of regulatory authorities. It must monitor those financial institutions operating in or from Dominica and take necessary action and liaise with and assisted by the FIU in the discharge of its functions. The Unit is endowed with information gathering and enforcement powers backed by criminal sanctions.

Director of Public Prosecutions

The Director of Public Prosecution, whose office is established by the Constitution, is in control of public prosecutions and in the excise of the powers of that office shall not, under section 72 (6), be subject to 'the direction and control of any other person or authority' and therefore the launching and prosecution of criminal cases is insulated from direct political influence (Telford Georges, 1999). Though a proviso in section 72 (2) requires that in discontinuing criminal proceedings he must act in accordance with directions (if any) that the Attorney General may give him. The ODPP is staffed by attorneys specialising in prosecuting complex cases and receives administrative support from the minister responsible for legal affairs. While criminal investigations are conducted by the police, criminal prosecutions are under the directions of the DPP.

Central Procurement Board

Section 8 of the *Public Procurement and Contract Administration Act* established a Central Procurement Board responsible for the administration of procurement procedures, including the award of contracts and the selection or suspension or debarment of contractors. The Board consists of six members: the Financial Secretary (Chairman), the Director of Trade, a legal officer from the ministry responsible for legal affairs, a senior officer of the Ministry of Finance, the Chief Technical Officer of the Ministry of Works and a representative of the Dominica Association of Industry and Commerce. The Act, at section 13 also set up a Central Procurement Unit within the Ministry of Finance, headed by a Chief Procurement Officer to administer the provisions of the Act.

The Board is mandated to strive to achieve the highest standards of transparency and equity in the execution of its duties and to submit an annual report to the Minister for Finance and copy the Director of Audit within six months of the close of each financial year. Immediately after the expiration of 30 days from the date of submission of the copy of the report to the Minister, the Board shall cause the report to be published on the government website.

Customs Department

The Customs Department provides support for anti-money laundering control activities and works closely with the FIU in that regard.

Dominica Police Service

The police are primarily responsible for investigations into crimes. They collaborate closely with oversight bodies in conducting investigations and enforcement of their regulatory functions.

6. Support for and Performance of Anti-Corruption Bodies

The vigour of government support for and the consistency of its commitment to the fight against corruption is critical for any measure of success to be achieved. All three political parties have committed to taking strong action to combat corruption. There is, therefore, consensus in Parliament as to the objective of safeguarding the society from the corrosive and debilitating effects of corruption.

Government continues to provide all the oversight bodies identified in this report with adequate budgets to finance their operations. In the case of the Integrity Commission, the Director of Audit and the DPP, in keeping with their status as independent bodies, budgets in respect of their offices are provided by law.

The print media in Dominica continues to play an important role, is relatively free and independent and boldly highlights issues surrounding mismanagement of public affairs. The role of social media has also gained traction in recent years.

The major institutions established to administer anti-corruption laws have performed creditably and have carried out their mandate, notwithstanding the many challenges deriving from deficiencies in legislation and other governance factors.

The Office of the Director of Audit dutifully submitted its reports for the financial years 2007–2018 to the Minister of Finance to satisfy the provisions of the Constitution and the *Audit Act* and consistently brought to public notice the Audit Department's concerns about the financial management of the affairs of the country over these fiscal years. In the June 2008 report, for example, the Director exposed a most unfavourable contract and advised that the Accounting Officer must do everything legally possible to have the estimated extraordinary gain of EC$557,783.00 realised in this transaction refunded to the Consolidated Fund. The Report pointed out 'that Government did not receive value for money as garbage bins of lesser quantity and value were received' by the Department under this contract. In July 2009, a substantial refund of the sum was made to the Consolidated Fund by a company controlled by a close relative of a sitting Minister. These annual reports, however, are invariably presented to the Minister of Finance some three years after the close of the June financial year and tabled in Parliament some six months later. The last meeting of the Public Accounts Committee on these accounts was held in 2015.

The FIU has built up capacity since its establishment with external assistance and, in its report for the year 2012, drew attention to substantial success in its money laundering control activities. The Unit has been able to augment its capabilities by forging strategic alliances with appropriate external institutions and corresponding regional bodies.

The Integrity Commission has also kept up with its mandate to receive declarations on the financial affairs of persons in public life and to investigate and report on any breach of its Code of Conduct or other acts of corruption. The Commission's annual reports for 2017–2020 were only laid in Parliament on 26 April 2021. The Commission was also able to strengthen its reporting mandate through the *Integrity in Public Office (Amendment) Act 2015,* which enabled it to submit its report directly to the Speaker of the House of Assembly in the event of failure to do so on the part of the minister responsible for legal affairs. It was also able to obtain enhanced authority to require the filing of declarations by applying to the High Court *ex parte* for an order directing the person in public life to file a declaration in addition to criminal sanctions.

Through its outreach programmes to gain public understanding and support, the Commission has also initiated effective measures to engage with public officials and the public, including:

- Sessions with persons in public life, including ministers and other parliamentarians to sensitise them concerning their statutory obligations and to explain the most important provisions of the Act and how these pertained to them.

- A press conference to interact with the media on the workings of the Commission and its performance and challenges.

- Engagement with the private sector on the purpose and functions of the Integrity Commission.

- Publication of articles concerning aspects of the provisions of the Act to build public awareness of and gain support for their implementation.

- Publication of a 'Questions and Answers Booklet' for the information of the public and persons in public life.

- Establishment of a website to disseminate information concerning the Commission and the carrying out of its functions and publication of its annual reports as soon as tabled in House of Assembly and media notification of same

The Commission also became a founding member of the Commonwealth Caribbean Association of Integrity Commissions and Anti-Corruption Bodies (CCAICACB), which was founded in 2015 to bring all anti-corruption professional bodies in the region together to organise common, focused and targeted assistance to member countries. The Association's clear strategy is 'to use the network of community of practice approach to suppress corruption in member states.

All the anti-corruption institutions have reported high levels of cooperation with the customs, police and ODPP. The FIU has specifically benefitted from its close alliance with counterpart regional bodies.

7. Lessons, Challenges, Conclusion and Recommendations

7.1 Lessons

The challenges faced and the successes achieved since the inception of the Integrity Commission and other recently established oversight bodies have left valuable lessons:

- Given the public clamour for bringing into force the *Integrity in Public Office Act 2003* and the establishment of an independent and impartial Commission, the appointing authorities (the Prime Minister and the Leader of the Opposition) in September 2008 did the right thing in advising the appointment of qualified, highly experienced and independent-minded persons to perform the intrusive investigatory duties and functions under the legislation.

- Many of the persons from the media and attorneys who were interviewed, however, expressed disquiet at the composition of the Commission established under the *Integrity in Public Office (Amendment) Act 2015* with a quorum that may constitute the two persons appointed by the Prime Minister, given the Commission's independent and intrusive jurisdiction over the Executive.

- Experience over the past 20 years has shown that improvements in the legislative framework and enhancements to administrative procedures are not a sufficient condition for sustaining anti-corruption policies. In the case of the Public

Accounts Committee, delays in the submission of the reports of the Director of Audit together with the government accounts have hampered its functioning and contributed to the infrequency of its meetings.

- Regular reviews of the legislative framework for oversight bodies help to maintain the relevance and effectiveness of the functions they were set up to carry out. The United Nations Conference of States Parties, 2015, in its report on Dominica, made extensive recommendations for legislative changes to create a more robust regime for its oversight bodies. The Integrity Commission in its several reports from 2008 to 2015 also made recommendations to strengthen its mandate and encourage public response to its operations. These legislative reviews, if attended to, would enhance the effectiveness of these oversight bodies in the fight against corruption.

- Similarly, institution strengthening of the several agencies is of utmost importance. A degree of autonomy should be allowed in the recruitment of staff and in budgetary support for their operations. Even so, Dominica's Integrity Commission on its own can hardly provide the quality of resources to sustain effective surveillance over public sector behaviour in all the areas covered by its legislation, and it could benefit from further regional cooperation and support in its operations. At the local level, the optimization of coordination among relevant agencies would bolster their collective strength to achieve the objectives for which they were established.

- Constant parliamentary oversight bolstered by the operations of well-ordered and coordinated oversight bodies is the most effective bulwark against corruption in all its forms.

7.2 Challenges

In its 11th Annual Report 2019, the Integrity Commission identified some of the challenges faced in the exercise of its functions, including 'the backlog of matters to be completed, the stability of the information system used for analysis, secure venue for meetings and having the full set of skills required for the effective examination of declarations. These challenges are interrelated …'

Report of Receipts of Gifts: In its 2019 and 2020 reports tabled in the House of Assembly on 26 April 2021, the Commission stated that the amended provisions on the reporting of the acceptance of gifts by a person in public life introduced in the Act of 2015 has made the law 'unclear' in that it provides that the declarant is only required 'to report to the Commission within 30 days gifts received from another person valued at less than $1000', so that 'there is no duty to make such a report for gifts valued at more than $1000 which the Commission does not believe reflects the intention of Parliament'.

As a trans-shipment point for narcotics, Dominica is affected by the international narcotics market. The laundering of money made outside the country is a major issue, and for this reason Dominica is on the list of countries considered of 'primary concern' by the U.S. State Department's Bureau of International Narcotics and

Law Enforcement Affairs (2019). The presence of an unknown number of offshore financial institutions with no published beneficial ownership heightens that risk (Bak et al., 2019).

Two major disasters in 2015 and 2017 destroyed the greater part of the country's wealth and left a large segment of the population homeless and in distress. In response to emergency calls for relief and shelter, departures from constitutional provisions and regulatory procedures were occasioned. The major and immediate challenge is to restore the observance of established laws and regulations for the conduct of government business.

A recent amendment to the enabling legislation of the Integrity Commission requires that where the Commission is of the view that an investigation is necessary to ascertain whether, on a complaint accepted under section 31 and 32, a person in public life has breached the Code of Conduct, it must give that person an opportunity to make representation prior to deciding whether to hold an inquiry and shall not proceed on an inquiry other than in relation to an alleged breach as particularised in the original complaint. The Act of 2003 restricted the Commission to act only on complaints received and not on its own volition. The amendment, therefore, constitutes a further limitation on its authority to establish probity, integrity and accountability in public life.

The channel of communication between the Integrity Commission and Parliament is through the minister responsible for legal affairs. *The Integrity in Public Office (Amendment) Act, 2015* authorises the Commission to send its report directly to the Speaker if after three months the minister fails to lay it before Parliament. Notwithstanding, government policy requires that all matters for laying before Parliament must be sanctioned by Cabinet. The reports of the Commission, though submitted in accordance with the amended statutory provisions, are therefore subject to further delays. The 2018, 2019 and 2020 reports were tabled in the House of Assembly on 26 April 2021.

Public support for oversight bodies in general, and the Integrity Commission in particular, is also a crucial issue. Public awareness and understanding of the role and purpose of these institutions is at best superficial, and this is exacerbated by the deep divide between political communities and strong adherence to party loyalties. Except for a brief appearance in Dominica by Transparency International two decades ago, no similar civic group that could champion the success of these oversight bodies has emerged.

7.3 Conclusion and recommendations

Executive accountability to Parliament and the reporting duty of oversight and regulatory bodies

It is recommended that the Commonwealth Secretariat Public Sector Governance Division, together with the Commonwealth Parliamentary Association (CPA), should hold a webinar/seminar/workshop for parliamentarians and general managers and chairpersons of statutory oversight bodies on the role of Parliament as the apex oversight body, the supportive role of these bodies in good governance and the rationale and purpose of reporting to Parliament on the discharge of their statutory mandates. Alternatively, this should be placed on the agenda for the next meeting of the CCAICACB.

In order to strengthen Parliament's oversight role, it is recommended that the *Integrity Act* should include provisions that require the minister to carry out an independent review of the operation and effectiveness of the Integrity Commission every three years and submit a report to the House of Assembly. A Standing Committee under the Standing Orders should examine this report and annual reports of the oversight bodies on the performance of their statutory functions.

Article 5 of UNCAC requires State parties to periodically evaluate relevant legal instruments and administrative measures with a view to determining their adequacy to prevent and fight corruption. Section 16A of the *Corruption (Prevention) Act, 2001* of Jamaica provides for such a review by a Committee of Parliament.

Funding of political parties and electoral campaigns

Although not formally recognised under the Dominica Constitution, political parties, since their emergence in 1950s, have played and continue to play an important constitutional role. They provide the principal means by which individuals participate in representative democracy. They are the transmission belt for the development and carriage of policy into legislation and practice and perform interest-aggregation and interest-articulation functions in the political system. They have, however, remained like 'private clubs exercising political power' (Address by Professor Trevor Munro at Second Commonwealth Caribbean Regional Meeting of Heads of Integrity Commissions and Anti-corruption Bodies, 1st March, 2016). Given their role as instruments of democracy, cogent reasons have been advanced for a supervisory role by the state in prescribing rules for the way political parties and election campaigns are financed. Recommendations to this effect have been made by independent observer missions to Dominica and contained in principles of international good practice and binding treaties for upholding democracy and transparency, equality and accountability in the electoral process of democratic states, consistent with article 7 (3) of the UNCAC.

At the second meeting of the Heads of the CCAICACB in 2016, the *Representation of the People (Amendment) Act 2016* of Jamaica was discussed. This Amending Act broke some new ground in the fight against political corruption in the Commonwealth Caribbean relating to political parties, campaign finance and election management. Political parties in Jamaica now had to be registered and came under the regulatory framework of the Electoral Commission, to which they had to make available their annual financial accounts and membership. They were eligible for a level of reimbursement for political administration and campaign finance provided that they were certified to be in compliance with the Code of Political Conduct, which included non-intimidation and non-inflammatory language.

The Government of Dominica has engaged the Rt. Hon. Sir Dennis Byron to conduct a review of the country's electoral process, systems and laws with a view to making recommendations for meaningful reform that will improve the system. In response to Sir Dennis's invitation to stakeholders, recommendations have been made in the media and by interviewees and stakeholders for the enactment of political party and election campaign finance with robust oversight provisions for Dominica under the *House of Assembly (Elections) Act* and other applicable laws (Sun Newspaper – June 8, 2009).

It is recommended that Benchmark 7 – Political Lobbying, Financing, Spending and Elections – in section 3 of the Commonwealth Anti-Corruption Benchmarks (April 2021) be taken on board by the Sir Dennis Byron Commission.

Strengthening of the Integrity Commission

In constituting oversight bodies such as the Integrity Commission, the appointing authority must consistently endeavour to appoint persons who are suitably qualified and possessed of the necessary experience and capacity to perform the high statutory purpose of advancing probity, integrity and accountability over powerful and high-level state functionaries. Such appointees must be persons not known to have strong and active political affiliation:

> 'Whatever official or institution administers the Act, they must be independent and seen to be independent and made up of Commissioners of good standing and reputation with the necessary skills to discharge effectively the ethical, legal, accounting and enforcement obligation imposed on them' (Commonwealth Secretariat, 2017).

The concerns raised by the Commission in its Annual Report of 2019 that the Secretariat does not have 'the full set of skills required for the effective examination of the declarations' of persons in public life has to be seen in the context of the command of Parliament under section 49 (1) of the Act that the Executive shall provide the Commission with a staff 'adequate for the prompt and efficient discharge of its functions under the Act'.

In its Annual Report 2011, the Commission published its recommendations to the Minister as follows:

> 'The Commission's experience in the discharge of its functions under the Act over the past years has forcefully revealed that comprehensive investigations into the financial affairs of persons in public life require high level management staff and professional staff in the field of forensic and investigative accountancy' (Integrity Commission of the Commonwealth of Dominica, 2011, p. 70).

A Country Procurement Assessment Report by the World Bank noted that,

> 'Art. 49 of the Act requires that the Commission has adequate staff to carry out its assigned responsibilities. It is critical that high level professional staff with legal and auditing background and familiarity with procurement be hired and adequately paid. As it is unlikely that local staff with significant skills and

experience can be identified, it is essential that the new staff receive substantial training on administrative and enforcement of ethical systems including appropriate forensic auditing and other investigative techniques.' (World Bank, 2003)

A fundamental pillar for an efficient and effective anti-corruption body is the possession of high-level professional staff who are loyal to it and its mandate. The 'Model Act on Integrity in Public Life' – a model particularly for small Commonwealth jurisdictions – recommended that the Commission be empowered to employ staff and engage on contract professional technical assistance to undertake investigations (Commonwealth Secretariat, 2017). Similar provisions are contained in section 7(1), (2) and (3) of the *Prevention of Corruption Act, 2007* of Belize. It is therefore recommended that the minimum staff complement and accountability to the Commission should be included in the enabling legislation.

There is an urgent need to a further amendment to the *Integrity Act* (Sec 48 (4)) to provide that the annual report when transmitted to the Speaker "shall be laid on the table of the House of Assembly by the Speaker at the next sitting following the receipt of the report", as provided in section 35 of the *Dominica Air and Seaport Authority Act*.

Bibliography

Print and online publications

Astaphan, A (2000) 'First Preliminary Report'. – a preliminary investigation into allegations of corruption, breach of trust, conflict of interest and misfeasance in public office directed against the previous United Workers Party administration – 11th. August, 2000 (Available at Documentation Centre, Kennedy Avenue, Roseau.)

Bak, M, M Jenkins and S Lemaitre (2019) 'Overview of Corruption and Anti-Corruption in Antigua and Barbuda, Barbados, Dominica, Guyana, Jamaica, St Lucia and Trinidad and Tobago'. Transparency International. www.jstor.com/stable/resrep20499

Commonwealth Secretariat (2017) 'Model Act on Integrity in Public Life'. London: Office of Civil and Criminal Justice Reform, Commonwealth Secretariat. https://production-new-commonwealth-files.s3.eu-west-2.amazonaws.com/migrated/key_reform_pdfs/P15370_1_ROL_Model_Act_Integrity.pdf

Commonwealth Secretariat/GIACC (Global Infrastructure Anti-Corruption Centre)/RICS (Royal Institute for Chartered Surveyors) 2021 *Commonwealth Anti-Corruption Benchmarks*. London: Commonwealth Secretariat. https://giaccentre.org/chess_info/uploads/2021/04/COMMONWEALTH-BENCHMARKS.APRIL-2021.pdf

Conference of the State Parties to the United Nations Conference against Corruption (2015) 'Implementation Review Group Sixth Session'. 1–5 June, Vienna. CAC/COSP/IRG/I/2/1/Add.30

Financial Intelligence Unit (2012) 'Annual Report'. Available at House of Assembly, Victoria Street, Roseau, Dominica.

Global Finance – https://www.gfmag.com/global-data/country-data/dominica -gdp-country-report

Government of the Commonwealth of Dominica (2015) 'Rapid Damage and Impact Assessment Tropical Storm Erika, August 27, 2015: A Report by the Government of Dominica'. 25 September. https://reliefweb.int/sites/reliefweb.int/files/ resources/Dominica-Rapid-Damage-and-Needs-Assessment.pdf

Government of the Commonwealth of Dominica (n.d.) 'National Resilience Development Strategy, Dominica 2030'. https://dominica.gov.dm/images/ documents/national_resilience_development_strategy_2030.pdf

Government of the Commonwealth of Dominica (2018) '2018 Budget: From Survival to Sustainability and Success – A Resilient Dominica'. Presented by Hon. Roosevelt Skerrit, Prime Minister and Minister of Finance, 25 July. https://finance.gov.dm/ budget/budget-addresses/file/27-budget-address-2018-2019-from-suarvival-to-sustainability-and-success-a-resilient-dominica

Heritage Foundation – https://www.heritage.org/index/pdf/2021/countries/.... PDF file

Includes Dominica real Gross Domestic Product growth rate, with latest forecasts and historical data, GDP per capita, GDP composition and breakdown by sector. Browse additional economic.

Integrity Commission of the Commonwealth of Dominica (2011) 'Third Annual Report: Year Ended August 31, 2011'. https://integritycommission.gov.dm/ reports/file/11-the-integrity-commission-third-annual-report-2011

Johnson, J (1985) 'The Doctrine of Ministerial Responsibility and Role and Functions of the Permanent Secretary in Dominica'. Currently held in bound volume at UWI Faculty of Law Library, Cavehill Campus, Thesis Collection.

Johnson, J (2011), 'Finance Administration: Public Procurement: Value For Money Accounting and Oversight Responsibility'. Sun Newspaper, 21 and 28 March and 4, 11 and 18 April. 2011.

Johnson, J (2021) 'Electoral Reform in Dominica, Political Party and Election Campaign Finance', Paper submitted to the Rt. Hon. Denis Byron, Dominica's Election Laws Review Commissioner (Unpublished).

McKoy, D (2012) Corruption: Law, Governance and Ethics in the Commonwealth Caribbean. Watton-at-Stone, UK: Hansib Publications.

Miller, T, AB Kim and JM Roberts (2021) 2021 Index of Economic Freedom. Washington, DC: The Heritage Foundation. https://www.heritage.org/index/ pdf/2021/book/index_2021.pdf

Munro, Trevor: Combatting Corruption More Effectively in the Caribbean – The Role of the CCAICACD, https://ccaicacb.org/web/Reports

Office of the Director of Audit (2008–2017) Director of Audit Reports for the Financial Year. audit.gov.dm

'Report of the Commission of Inquiry into the Public Works Department of Dominica (1963)'. Portsmouth: Grosvenor Press. (Available at Documentation Center, Kennedy Avenue, Roseau).

Rutter, J (2013) 'The Strange Case of Non-Ministerial Departments'. Institute for Government. https://www.instituteforgovernment.org.uk/sites/default/files/publications/NMDs%20-%20final.pdf

Telford Georges, P (1999), 'Report of the Constitution Review Commission'. Roseau: Government Printery.

United Nations Office on Drugs and Crime (2015) 'Country Review Report on the Commonwealth of Dominica 2015'. https://www.unodc.org/wdr2015

World Bank (2003) 'Commonwealth of Dominica: Country Procurement Assessment Report'. https://documents1.worldbank.org/curated/en/358191468746802249/pdf/3097510v111DM.pdf

World Bank (2020) 'World Development Indicators Data Base'. https://databank.worldbank.org/source/world-development-indicators

Legislation

Audit Act, Chap. 63:01

Automatic Exchange of Financial Account Information (Common Reporting Standard) Act, 2019 (No. 6 of 2019)

Commonwealth of Dominica Constitution Order: Standing Orders of the House of Assembly Chap 1:10

Commonwealth of Dominica Citizenship by Investment Regulations, Chap 1:10

Customs Act, Chap. 69:01

Dominica Air and Sea Ports Authority Act, Chap. 50:01

Exchange of Information Act, Chap. 20:05

Finance (Administration) Act, Chap. 63:02

Finance Intelligence Unit Act, Chap. 63:04

Financial Services Unit Act, Chap. 63:03

House of Assembly (Elections) Act, Chap. 2:01

Integrity in Public Office Act, Chap. 23:04

International Maritime Act, Chap. 48:01

Money Laundering (Prevention) Act, Chap. 73:01

Proceeds of Crime Act, Chap. 12:29

Public Procurement and Contract Administration Act, Chap. 63:06

Public Service Act, Chap. 23:01

Sharing of Intelligence Among Member States of the Caribbean Community Act, Chap. 13:12

Suppression of the Financing of Terrorism Act, Chap. 73:04

Transitional Organized Crime (Prevention and Control) Act, Chap. 14:02

Persons Interviewed

House of Assembly

–   Speaker of the House

–   Clerk of the House

–   Leader of the Opposition/Chairman of the Public Accounts Committee

Integrity Commission

–   Chairman and members

–   Senior staff

Members of the Former Commission

Secretary to the Cabinet and Head of the Public Service

Comptroller of Inland Revenue Division

Former Attorneys General

Former Financial Secretaries

Accountant General

Dominica Bar Association

Committee of Concerned Lawyers

Director of Audit

Editor, Sun Newspaper

Freelance Journalist and Editor of Nature Isle News Services

General Secretary, Public Service Union

Joint Consultative Committee on the Construction Sectors (Chairman)

Former Deputy Leader UWP/Former Minister for Finance (UWP)

Former Minister for Economic Development (DLP) and Vice President (DLP)

Former Chief of Police

Former Superintendent of Police

Chapter 5

Grenada

Colin McDonald PhD

Abstract

After some challenges during the late 1990s and the early part of the 2000s, the Government of Grenada moved decisively to strengthen institutional arrangements to address corruption and promote good governance. There was the enactment of a plethora of legislation, the establishment of new organizations and the acceptance of regional and International standards by the Government aimed at addressing corruption. Generally, there is an 'average' perception in Grenada as it relates to the level of corruption within the public sector but a low perception of corruption within the private sector. The perception data present what can be called an 'uncertain corruption environment', one in which there is less confidence among individuals to engage in corrupt behaviour. Effectively this means Grenada is less inviting for politicians and public officers who may want to engage in corruption. The uncertain corruption environment suggests Grenada's Corruption Perception Index (CPI) score can be partly explained by accepted societal norms, beliefs and values. However, Grenada's score on the Corruption Perception Index (CPI) has slipped from 56 to 53 over the period 2016–2020, and the country cannot become complacent in its fight against corruption.

1. Introduction and Background

As part of the research on combatting corruption in the Caribbean, this chapter focuses on the factors and institutions in Grenada that have contributed to the reduction of the impact of corruption and the elements that have enabled it to implement successful anti-corruption strategies.

The project is more than timely when viewed within the wider context of governance. Its usefulness is reflected in the comments of Grenade (2012, p. 54), who stated,

> 'Today, Caribbean citizens generally enjoy political rights and civil liberties, state institutions function well, and there are regular constitutional transfers of power through multiparty elections. However, despite the trappings of formal democracy, there are grave deficiencies that undermine effective governance in the Caribbean. These include excessive prime-ministerial powers, an electoral system that is prone to distortions, clientelism, and an alienated citizenry. When taken together, those issues can breed corruption and undermine governance.'

Within this context, and given that corruption is an issue in the Caribbean, this project aims to unearth issues that have the overall potential to improve governance and strengthen the anti-corruption agenda in the region. The research involved the following tasks:

- Reviewing the existing literature on efforts to combat corruption in Grenada;

- Making a field visit to the country and conducting extensive interviews with key stakeholders in government, civil society, development partners and the private sector;

- Identifying organisations or institutions that are driving the anti-corruption effort; and

- Utilising any other appropriate research methodologies, including telephone interviews, focus group studies and surveys of key stakeholders to gain access to the information required.

Against this background the report will:

- Identify the impact made by key institutions involved in the fight against corruption;

- Discuss the extent to which these institutions have been able to facilitate a whole-of-government approach to combatting corruption;

- Investigate how government institutions have worked with groups such as political parties, civil society organisations, the media, development partners and the private sector in the course of their anti-corruption efforts; and

- Discuss how lessons from the country's study could be applied elsewhere in Commonwealth Caribbean.

In 2021, Transparency International stated with regard to its Corruption Perception Index (CPI) that,

> 'Like previous years, more than two-thirds of countries score below 50 on this year's CPI, with an average score of just 43. The data shows that despite some progress, most countries still fail to tackle corruption effectively. In addition to earning poor scores, nearly half of all countries have been stagnant on the CPI for almost a decade. These countries have failed to move the needle in any significant way to improve their score and combat public sector corruption.' (Transparency International, 2021, p. 6)

In this context, Grenada has done comparatively well given its relatively strong scores on the CPI over the last five years (see Table 1). Every year its scores are well above the average and the country is certainly not 'stagnant on the CPI'. It is also important to note that the report also states that, 'With an average score of 43 for the fifth consecutive year, the Americas showcases corruption and the mismanagement of funds in one of the regions most affected by the COVID-19 crisis' (ibid.). However, over the period 2016–2020 Grenada's score has slipped from 56 to 53. This certainly means the country cannot become complacent in its fight against corruption.

Table 1. Grenada's position on the Corruption Perceptions Index, 2016–2020

Year	Score	Rank
2016	56	46
2017	52	52
2018	52	53
2019	53	51
2020	53	52

2. Review Methodology

The research methods included:

1. Secondary data collection: the review of pertinent documents.

2. Primary data collection: interviews and virtual stakeholder group interviews and discussions.

Data collection was guided by the following operating principles:

1. A wealth of information exists on the central theme – anti-corruption – within the Caribbean and the wider Commonwealth and, wherever feasible, the research generated by previous studies in this area would be utilised and built on;

2. Fresh research would be undertaken to fill gaps and address the relevant issues; and

3. Full use would be made of modern communication technologies so as to minimise costs and time.

The first step was to review existing materials and develop a basic understanding of the issues surrounding anti-corruption, particularly in Grenada. This phase also involved the identification of key stakeholders and institutions driving the anti-corruption agenda. It was the beginning of data gathering, including all relevant studies, reports and related material.

Interviews were then held guided by questionnaires as well as discussions guided by a checklist. One questionnaire was used to interview internal stakeholders, while another questionnaire and a checklist were used to interview other stakeholders, the media and civil society organisations. In addition to interviews with internal stakeholders, there were lengthy discussions with some of them (see Appendices A and B).

Based on this research, the report discusses the elements that are necessary to promote anti- corruption measures and good governance. It also makes recommendations, flowing from the analysis, on appropriate policy as well as the legal and regulatory framework to reduce corruption and facilitate good governance. The focus of the report is on what worked as opposed to what did not work; workable institutional arrangements as opposed to institutional weaknesses; and, even more importantly, what positive lessons were learnt that can be transferrable to other Commonwealth jurisdiction in the fight against corruption.

3. Socio-Economic and Political Context

3.1 Political structure

The Caribbean state of Grenada is made up of three islands: Grenada, Carriacou and Petit Martinique. A former British colony, the country gained its independence in 1974 and has been a member of the Commonwealth since that time. It occupies an area of approximately 131 sq. miles and in 2020 was home to an estimated population of 112,933 citizens (Worldometer, 2022). The major ethnic grouping is African descendants (82.4 per cent), with mixed ethnicity accounting for 13.3 per cent and East Indians for 2.3 per cent. Other ancestry at 1.35 per cent make up the remainder of the population.

Under the 1973 Constitution, Grenada adopted a parliamentary-style democratic model with a Constitutional Monarch, Queen Elizabeth II, as the Head of State represented by the Governor General. The country is governed under a multi-party parliamentary system with the political and legal traditions closely following those of the United Kingdom; it has a prime minister, a cabinet and a bicameral Parliament with an elected House of Representatives and an appointed Senate. The Government is divided into three branches: legislative, executive and judicial.

With regard to the legislative branch, the Parliament consists of Her Majesty, the Senate and the House of Representatives. There are 15 elected members in the House of Representatives and 13 Senators. The judiciary is independent of the executive and the legislature, and jurisprudence is based on English common law. Grenada is a member of the Eastern Caribbean Supreme Court (ECSC) system, which is the superior court of the Organisation of Eastern Caribbean States (OECS). The ECSC, headquartered in St Lucia, consists of the Court of Appeal, headed by the Chief Justice and four Judges, and the High Court with 18 Judges. The former is itinerant, traveling to member States on a schedule to hear appeals from the High Court and subordinate courts; High Court judges reside in the various member States, with two residing in Grenada.

3.2 Economic structure

Grenada relies on tourism, agriculture and revenue generated by St George's University as its main sources of foreign exchange. The economy is largely tourism-based, small and open, therefore having a very high propensity to import. Over the past two decades, the main thrust of the economy has shifted from agriculture to services, with tourism serving as the leading foreign currency-earning sector. The principal export crops are nutmeg and mace (Grenada is the world's second largest producer of nutmeg after Indonesia). Other crops for export include cocoa, citrus fruits, bananas, cloves and cinnamon. Manufacturing industries in Grenada operate mostly on a small scale, including production of beverages and other foodstuffs, textiles and the assembly of electronic components for export. The composition of its gross domestic product (GDP) by sector of origin are as follows: agriculture, 9.1 per cent; industry, 14.2 per cent; and services, 76.7 per cent.

As is the case in most islands in the Caribbean, the Government is the largest single employer. "Public service employees are categorised as follows: permanent establishment, contract officers and temporary (open vote) staff. It has been observed that there has been a growing tendency to employ contract officers labour from outside the traditional public service under what is described as 'flexible mechanisms in order to deliver services' and this has had mixed results" (Kirton, 2011, p. 9)

The Department of Public Administration (DPA) is charged with the responsibility of 'introducing and sustaining modern human resource management practices in the Public Service' and its mission statement embraces the commitment to the enhancement of the delivery of public services in Grenada in an efficient and effective manner through the modern management systems and practices. Some of these improvements were highlighted in the *Doing Business 2011* report,

> 'Grenada eased business start-up by transferring responsibility for the commercial registry from the courts to the civil administration. The appointment of a registrar focusing only on property cut the time needed to transfer property in Grenada by almost half. Grenada's customs administration made trading faster by simplifying procedures, reducing inspections, improving staff training and enhancing communication with users.' (World Bank, 2010, pp. 136–137)

Within this context, there are ongoing efforts to close the existing gaps through digitalization of procedures. Grenada is ranked 146 among 190 economies in the *Doing Business 2020* report (World Bank, 2020).

Improved labour market institutions are needed to match job opportunities with Grenada's still-young labour force. Upgrading education, training programmes and employment-matching services (through well-functioning central depository of labour market data) should help tap into this potential.

In 2020, Grenada suffered a major contraction in its economy due to the COVID-19 pandemic, which has further compounded the situation of high unemployment of above 20 per cent in recent years. Although this was partly related to the impact of the global economic downturn, unemployment was already high before this, suggesting there are structural factors behind it. According to the International Monetary Fund (IMF), another explanation could be,

> 'the significant decline in the banana and sugar industries in the 1990s is usually cited as a major shock on labor demand that likely fueled structural unemployment in some ECCU (Eastern Caribbean Currency Union) countries. Until the mid-1990s, exports of both products in African, Caribbean and Pacific (ACP) countries enjoyed preferential access to protected European markets, allowing them to sell these products at relatively high prices. Successive reforms to the European Union's regime since then phased out these preferences, triggering a gradual collapse of ECCU's banana/sugar exports.' (IMF, 2019, p. 13)

4. Legal and Institutional Backing for Anti-Corruption Efforts

As important as the policies and resources for development are, the institutions within which public action is embedded – the 'rules of the game' and the mechanisms through which they are monitored and enforced – are even more important. Institutions can include organisational rules and routines, formal laws and informal norms. Together they shape the incentives of public policymakers, overseers and providers of public services (World Bank, 1997).

During the late 1990s and early part of 2000s, such institutional arrangements and policies were not present in Grenada to oversee its financial sector. As such, to many, the island was then seen as a haven for Ponzi schemes and fraudulent off-shore banking transactions. It was a period during which the country suffered much reputational damage. The offshore banking scandal began shortly after Grenada licensed its first offshore bank in 1997. It went on to license approximately 40 banks, most of which had collapsed by 2003. During this period, 'St George's was headquarters to one of the most outlandish banking frauds, in which US and Canadian retirees were defrauded of millions while local officials looked the other way' (Woodard, 2008).

However, in January 2002, the Government reaffirmed its commitment to the inter-American system by ratifying a series of Organization of American States (OAS) conventions on the fight against corruption, terrorism and arms trafficking: the Inter-American Convention against Corruption (IACAC), the Convention against the Illicit Manufacturing of and Trafficking in Firearms, the Convention to Prevent and Punish Acts of Terrorism and the Inter-American Convention on Mutual Assistance in Criminal Matters.

The country began to transform its legal and institutional framework so as to address corruption and promote good governance. Woodard (2008) wrote that,

> 'Now Grenada is preparing to reopen its offshore financial services sector six years after it collapsed in a wave of international criminal investigations, trials, and allegations of government collusion. The country has replaced its fractured regulatory regime with a single organization to oversee all offshore activities, from insurance companies to credit services. The head of the new institution said this week that amended finance laws will allow the Attorney General authority to take immediate court action against any offshore entity suspected of fraud.'

There were a plethora of new laws, policies and institutional changes all aimed at creating an appropriate institutional framework to facilitate financial transactions and rein in corrupt individuals.

4.1 The legal system

The *Prevention of Corruption Act No.15 of 2007* aims 'to make provision of the prevention of corruption practices by Public officers in the performance of public functions, to give effect to the provision of the OAS Inter American Convention

Against Corruption and for matters connected thereto and for purposes connected therewith'. It states that,

> 'corruption means an act committed by a person that is inconsistent with his or her lawful duties and the rights of others, by unlawfully and wrongfully using his or her influence, office or character to procure some gratification for himself or herself or for another person and includes bribery, fraud and other related offences; and the term 'corrupt' shall have a corresponding meaning'.

This expanded view of corruption seems to suggest the Government's commitment to address all forms and shades of corruption and maladministration.

The 2007 Act was repealed and updated by the *Integrity in Public Life Act No. 24. of 2013*. It is responsible for ensuring integrity in public life, obtaining declaration of the assets, liabilities, income and interest in relation to property of persons in public life, to give effect to the provisions of the IACAC and matters incidental to and purposes connected to this. It requires that all public servants report their income and assets to an independent integrity commission for review. The first members of the Grenada Integrity Commission (GIC) were sworn in on January 2010.

This Act in turn was amended by the *Integrity in Public Life Amendment Act No.5 of 2015*. This provides for the GIC to receive and verify the accuracy of declarations of financial affairs from public officials; to investigate complaints of impropriety, corruption and misconduct by public officials; and for prosecution of persons found guilty of crimes according to the Acts. The Director of Public Prosecution (DPP) is the chief investigator under the *Prevention of Corruption Act* and therefore involved in the investigations of the Commission.

The *Financial Intelligence Act No. 14 of 2012* was enacted to make provision for the establishment of the Financial Intelligence Unit (FIU) for the investigation, detection, prevention and control of financial crimes and for connected matters. This Act also works alongside the *Proceeds of Crime Act, No. 6 of 2012* and the *Terrorism Act 16 of 2012*.

Under the *Proceeds of Crime Act No. 6 of 2012*, 'criminal conduct' means: (a) drug trafficking, or (b) any relevant offence. 'Relevant offence' means: (a) any indictable offence, or offence triable both summarily or on indictment in Grenada, from which a person has benefitted other than a drug trafficking offence; (b) any act or omission which, had it occurred in Grenada, would have constituted an offence (c) any offence falling within the 'designated category of offences', outlined under the FATF Recommendations and contained in the Schedule. The *Terrorism Act. Act. No. 16 of 2012* makes provision to combat terrorism and terrorist financing. Amongst other things 'terrorism' means the use or threat of action where: (i) this is designed to influence the government or to intimidate the public or a section of the public; and (ii) this is made for the purpose of advancing a political, religious or ideological cause.

The *Fiscal Responsibility Act No. 29 of 2015* aims to establish a transparent and accountable rule-based fiscal responsibility framework in Grenada, to guide and anchor fiscal policy during the budget process to ensure that government finances are sustainable over the short, medium and long term, consistent with a sustainable level of debt, and for related matters. The objects of this Act are:

a. to ensure that fiscal and financial affairs are conducted in a transparent manner;

b. to ensure full and timely disclosure and wide publication of all transactions and decisions involving public revenues and expenditures and their implications;

c. to ensure that debt is reduced to, and then maintained at, a prudent and sustainable level by maintaining primary surpluses that are consistent with this object; and

d. to ensure prudent management of fiscal risks.

The Act created a Fiscal Responsibility Oversight Committee (FROC).

The *Public Procurement and Disposal of Public Property Act No. 39 of 2014* aims to promote the public interest by prescribing the principles of good governance namely accountability, transparency, integrity and value for money in public procurement and to establish a framework of operational principles and procedures for efficient public procurement and for the disposal of public property by public entities and to provide for other related matters to achieve the following objectives:

a. maximise economy and efficiency;

b. promote competition among suppliers, contractors, consultants and service providers and provide for their fair, equal and equitable treatment;

c. promote the integrity and fairness of such procedures;

d. increase transparency and accountability in such procedures;

e. increase public confidence in such procedures; and

f. facilitate the promotion of local industry and economic development.

Departments within the Ministry of Finance are directly involved in and also oversee the procurement process within the public sector. In addition, the Audit Department has oversight responsibility for all procurement matters in the public sector. Its mission statement is 'to bring about good government through the promotion of greater accountability and transparency'. In addition, the Department's objective and purpose are stated as 'to develop a cadre of highly motivated and professional staff providing the best quality of audit service to the State'.

The Public Procurement and Disposal of Public Property Regulations, 2015 specifically addresses key issues that make for an open and transparent procurement system. In terms of oversight and institutional arrangements, the Act is very specific on matters of structure, operational principles and processes, decision-making rights and evaluation and selection criteria. For example, it states in part under Oversight by the Board that, 'the Board shall have responsibility for every procurement of goods, works and services, where the value of such procurement exceeds the approval threshold of $1,000,000, whether the procuring entity is a state-controlled enterprise, a statutory body or otherwise'.

In terms of approval thresholds, the Regulations state in part,

'(1) The approval thresholds for methods of procurement, the authorisation levels for awards of contract and for the signing of contracts shall be as set down in these Regulations and the procurement procedures. (2) Where the value of a proposed procurement does not exceed the approval threshold of $200,000, the chief accountable officer of the procuring entity shall be the approving authority and shall sign the procurement contract. (3) Where the value of a proposed procurement exceeds the approval threshold under sub-regulation (2), prior to execution of a notification of an award letter and a procurement contract, the Chief Accountable Officer of the procuring entity shall review the Tender Evaluation Report and submit to the Board (a) the Tender Evaluation Report; (b) his or her written comments; and (c) all other required documentation to the Board, for the issuance of a Certificate of Formal Approval or a Certificate of 'No Objection' to Contract Award pursuant to regulation 5.'

In terms of responsibilities, the Act identifies a Chief Accountable Officer responsible for (a) appointing a tender committee for procurement of goods, works and services, where the value is between the approval thresholds of $15,000 and $1,000,000; (b) establishing a procurement unit; (c) signing contracts on behalf of the procuring entity for procurement and disposal activities for contracts; (d) preparing the procurement plans; and (e) keeping and managing proper records of procurement proceedings.

The World Bank (2020, p. 71) states that,

'At a minimum, governments need to perform the following six procedures to award a public contract:

1. Communicate the opportunity to the private sector;

2. Collect the bids;

3. Open all bids received;

4. Evaluate the bids and award the contract;

5. Sign the contract; and

6. Authorize the beginning of the works.'

All of these are clearly addressed in the Act, which also establishes timeframes for certain actions and procedures. For example, the Act states that, 'Every Tenders Evaluation Report shall be approved by the chief accountable officer or the Board, as the case may be, within five business days of [its] receipt'. The Act also states that 'day' means a calendar day. Such a clause is clearly meant to place time limits on the tendering process and remove the possibility of delays. Tanzi (1998, p. 124) states,

'A further way to 'disturb' corruption is to reduce the opportunities to delay the total procedure or parts of it. A public official may profit on delays as continuation could depend on bribes. Strict time limits by which a given request must be rejected or accepted are therefore important to curb corruption, or to reduce the chance that public officials invite bribes by simply sitting on requests.'

The Act attempts to promote efficiency in awarding public contracts; it improves the level of competition and encourages participation of suppliers, which ensures better use of taxpayers' money. It also provides for a central procurement unit, a tender committee and an evaluation committee and outlines their composition and how they are to be appointed, their functions and responsibilities.

The *Freedom of Information Act, 2007* is intended to reinforce and give further effect to certain fundamental principles underlying the system of constitutional democracy: (a) governmental accountability; (b) transparency; and (c) public participation in national decision-making, by granting to the public a general right of access to official documents held by a public authority, subject to exemptions that balance that right against the public interest in exempting from disclosure governmental, commercial or personal information of a sensitive nature. The provision and access to pertinent information, along with the strengthening of legislative oversight, are likely to promote good governance and reduce corruption.

4.2 The institutional framework

Grenada Authority for the Regulation of Financial Institutions (GARFIN)

GARFIN was created by the *Regulation of Financial Institutions Act No. 5 of 2006*. This Act was repealed and replaced by Act. No. 1 of 2008, which broadened the scope of responsibilities of GARFIN and strengthened its supervisory powers. The mission of the Authority is to promote and maintain public confidence in, and the integrity of, the financial system in Grenada through the effective regulation and supervision of designated non- bank financial institutions. This includes supervising and regulating:

- Credit unions

- International companies

- Insurance companies

- Money services.

In effect, it is the single regulatory authority of the entire non-bank financial sector, thereby consolidating supervision for the administration of 12 pieces of legislation. It constantly supervises the activity of such entities in order to spot any wrongdoing, thus promoting accountability and openness. It has implemented a system of off-site and on-site supervision and conducted its first inspection of money services. Money value transfer (MVT) operators fall under the *Money Services Business Act,* and GARFIN has introduced quarterly reporting, submission of audited financial statements and site inspections as a means of monitoring MVT service operators.

Consolidation of supervision under one regulatory authority was designed to strengthen overall supervision of the sector. A careful reading of the Act indicates GARFIN is involved with four main activities as it undertakes its regulatory functions:

- Developing guidelines for money services businesses;

- Supervision of money services businesses;

- Licensing money service business; and

- Revocation of licenses from money services businesses.

The formation of GARFIN reflects a collaborative multidimensional approach involving structures, policies and procedures of varying key institutional frameworks. This approach indicates that from the inception the Government was aware that the fight against corruption needed a 'systems approach'. Such an approach lays the foundation for building organisations that can facilitate a whole-of-government approach to combatting corruption, thereby making such organisations fit for purpose.

The Grenada Integrity Commission (GIC)

The GIC's mandate is to:

- Carry out those functions and exercise the powers pursuant to the provisions of the *Integrity in Public life Act No.24 of 2013* and the *Prevention of Corruption Act No. 15 of 2007*;

- Receive and examine all declarations filed pursuant to the provisions of the Act;

- Make such inquiries as it considers necessary in order to verify or determine the accuracy of a declaration filed pursuant to the provisions of the Act;

- Receive and investigate complaints regarding any alleged breaches of the provisions or the commission of any suspected offence under the Act;

- Investigate the conduct of any person falling under the purview of the Commission which, in the opinion of the Commission, may be considered dishonest or conducive to corruption;

- Examine the practices and procedures of public bodies;

- Instruct, advise and assist the heads of public bodies with respect to changes in practices or procedures that may be necessary to reduce the occurrence of corrupt practices;

- Carry out programmes of public education intended to foster an understanding of the standard of integrity;

- Perform such other functions and exercise such powers as are required pursuant to the provisions of the Act.

In terms of the focus of the GIC's work, a review of its Annual Reports for the period 2014- 2019 indicates much emphasis is placed on the filing of asset declarations, by public officials. Table 2 indicates there is a high level of compliance on the part of officials.

The Commission's focus on asset declaration, along with the increase of officials making declarations, augers well for open, accountable and transparent government,

Table 2. Filing of declarations by public officers, 2018

Categories	Number of notices sent	Number of declarations filedmb	Outstanding declarations
Parliamentarians	12	10	2
Secretary to the Cabinet	1	1	0
Permanent Secretaries	13	13	0
Attorney General	1	0	1
Chief Magistrate & Legal Officers	13	12	1
Registrars of Corporate Affairs and Intellectual Property Office (CAIPO) & Supreme Court	2	2	0
Solicitor General	1	1	0
Director of Audit (Ag) & Senior Auditors	8	8	0
Comptroller and Deputy Comptroller of Inland Revenue	2	2	0
Chief Budget Officer	1	1	0
Senior Admin. Officers	7	7	0
Heads of Department & Senior Officers	44 (1 person retired prior to notice)	38	6
Deputy Accountant General (Ag)	1	1	0
Supervisor of Elections	1	1	0
Chief Procurement Officer	1	1	0
Chief Fisheries Officer	1	1	0
General Manager of Ports Auth.	1	1	0
Statutory Bodies	22 (1 person retired prior to notice)	16	8 (including 4 ex parte)
Royal Grenada Police Force (*flagged*)	8	8	0
Senior Police & Prison Officers	7	7	0
New Jr. Customs Officers	37	37	0
Total	**184**	**166**	**18**

Source: Office of the Integrity Commission (2018)'Fifth Annual Report'. St Georges, Grenada.

forms part of the fundamental principles that sustain the trust of the population and gives authority to executive powers of the state. The GIC has received on-site training by world experts of the UN Office on Drugs and Crime (UNODC) in international best practices in terms of the implementation of this function.

The GIC Annual Report 2019, under the heading 'Procedure for Handling Non-compliance', states,

'it has been noted that some declarants are blatantly ignoring the Commission even though the legislation is clear. In an effort to address this matter, a draft procedure for handling non-compliance was developed for the Commission's approval.' (p. 30)

This procedure was approved and is now a streamlined part of the declaration process. In addition, the Commission's website explains how to prepare the declaration form. Once declarations are received, they are quickly processed and then reviewed for compliance. The organic progression has led to speeding up of the overall process. Commenting on this issue, one interviewee stated,

> 'A lot has been done to educate the public on the realities and necessity for the work of the Commission. Further, the declaration process has become easier with time due to the level of awareness created to complete the process. However, persons view the declaration as an intrusion of privacy which limits their compliance.'

Another said,

> 'there has been improvement on public awareness and education which increased persons knowledge on the mandate of the Commission. Additionally, this boosted the level of declarations as persons became more amenable to the process.'

This improvement in declaration and compliance will go a very long way, given that it is effectively a way of monitoring declarants' financial and asset transactions. Monitoring when well done has tremendous potential to spur positive behavioural changes among its target group. Generally, there is a positive perception of the GIC among stakeholders. On a scale of 1 (low) to 10 (high), 57 per cent of interviewees/ stakeholders rated the GIC at 7 and 14 per cent rated it at 8. There were also positive comments such as 'GIC has been giving consistent messaging and is fully committed to high standards and accountability' from interviewees.

The GIC has undertaken a number of initiatives in the fight against corruption, including:

- Establishing a memorandum of understanding (MOU) with the Financial Intelligence Unit (FIU), which leads to the sharing of pertinent information

- Establishing an MOU with the Royal Grenada Police Force, with police officers being assigned to assist with the work of the Commission's Investigative Department

- Undertaking investigations that adopt a stakeholder approach where required

- Undertaking hearings and/or examining complaints against public officers and officials

- Undertaking joint training programmes with the FIU and the Procurement Department of the Ministry of Finance across the wider public service on topics relative to anti-corruption and good governance

- Developing an investigative system that is facilitated by an investigative tool

- Undertaking the training of all custom officers on matters relative to anti-corruption through what is called accelerated collaboration and training for investigation

- Advising that all custom officers within the island's public service have to make a declaration of their assets

- Identifying key stakeholders and, under the auspices of the Commonwealth Secretariat, launching its National Roundtable Anti-Corruption Mechanism, which facilitates an annual Roundtable on Anti-Corruption in which all key stakeholders participate

- Implementing a critical public education and outreach programme, through which presentations are made to ministries, departments, political parties, statutory bodies and schools

- Reviewing the draft policies on anti-corruption, conflict-of-Interest, fraud and bribery of the Grenada Industrial Development Corporation (GIDC). These policies have since been finalised and published by the GIDC and are the national best practice. Transparency International assisted with this initiative.

- Advising on the establishment of a gift register for public officers. Any gift received by a public officer in excess of EC$500 must be recorded in the gift register. Such declarations have already been received and processed.

A careful examination of these initiatives indicates a coordinated cross-organisational approach, which is in keeping with the whole-of-government approach to tackling corruption within the public sector. As stated by the Organisation for Economic Co-operation and Development (OECD),

> 'The whole-of-government approach to combating financial crime involves recognising that the activities of separate agencies do not operate in isolation. Officials in agencies including the tax administration, the customs administration, the FIU, the police and specialised criminal law enforcement agencies, the public prosecutor's office, authorities responsible for corruption investigations and financial regulators recognise that the knowledge and skills required to combat financial crime are often spread across each of these agencies.' (2017, p. 28)

Sharing of information between the GIC and the FIU is a necessary condition for inter-agency co-operation in combating corruption and financial crime and enables the agencies to work together to their mutual benefit. In addition to sharing information, it enables an investigation team to draw on a wider range of skills and experience from investigators with different backgrounds and training. Joint investigations may avoid duplication and increase efficiency by enabling officials from each agency to focus on different aspects of an investigation. The net effect of these measures and strategies is the creation of an environment that is less likely to facilitate corrupt behaviour by public officers.

The Financial Intelligence Unit (FIU)

The FIU is the primary institution in Grenada for conducting investigations concerning financial crimes. It has the responsibility to:

a. investigate all categories of financial crimes

b. collect information and maintain intelligence databases in relation to financial crimes

c. collect, analyse, assess and disseminate reports and information to bodies with similar objectives

d. develop and maintain a relationship with regional and international associations or organizations, with which it is required to share information

e. exercise its functions with due regard for the rights of citizens

f. ensure compliance with the *Proceeds of Crime Act, the Terrorism Act* and any other related enactment.

On 4 July 2011, Cabinet directed that the FIU be designated as the authority to which every financial institution would be required to report all currency transactions above the threshold of EC$50,000.00. In the fight against corruption, there is merit in implementing a system where financial institutions report transactions in currency above a prescribed threshold to a centralised national authority. In addition, the FIU has a working relationship with other relevant government agencies. A Technical Working Group has been created comprising the FIU, Customs, Police, Inland Revenue, Drug Unit, Special Branch and other agencies where discussions are held on financial and other matters and information sharing takes place. An MOU has been established to guide the operations of the Group, which meets once per month.

The successful performance of the FIU can be explained by its strategy, resources and execution. First, its strategy is collaborative, in that it works with all the key players along the 'corruption busting value chain'. Second, by working with the other entities the FIU has access to much more resources and specialised skills and competencies. Third, its execution is improved by efficient information flows across organizational boundaries and clear decision-making rights. Countering financial crimes require more effective intelligence gathering, analysis and sharing between government agencies to prevent, detect and prosecute criminals and recover the proceeds of their illicit activities. The FIU is structured and operates to do just that.

Central Procurement Unit

The potential for corruption through the procurement process in small island states such as Grenada is huge, given that the government is usually a large, if not the largest, purchaser of goods and services within the economy. Tanzi (1998) explains that one reason for corruption in developing and transition economies is that state rules and regulations provide the public officials with a monopoly authority that may prove useful to demand bribes. In order to reduce the level of bureaucratic corruption, it is therefore important to reduce this regulatory framework while improving, as well as executing, anti-corruption laws.

The *Public Procurement and Disposal of Public Property Act No. 39 of 2014* provides for a Procurement Unit and a Central Procurement Unit. In the case of the latter, it states in part that it shall,

'carry out any procurement on behalf of a Government department that has not been authorised as a procuring entity or pursuant to a request under regulation 8 (4), …prepare an annual procurement plan of every major item of expenditure for procurements envisaged to be purchased in any financial year, ... maintain records of particulars with respect to ad-hoc procurements in the format as provided by the Board. ... organise the purchase of common-use items either under individual contract arrangements or framework contract arrangements... [and] comply with the procurement procedures set down in these Regulations'.

Procurement was an area of much focus in discussions and interviews with individuals, and there was an observable contradiction. Even where interviewees rated the existing procurement system as average (5 or 6 on a score of 1 low to 10 high), they were quick to state, 'even though there is corruption generally, Grenadians are honest people'. Other similar comments were as follows:

'There is petty corruption'.

'Corruption is more popular in the public sector due to lack of monitoring and evaluation'.

'Corruption challenges are minuscule in Grenada. Our system appears to be working'.

'Corruption is due to lack of checks and balances in some instances'.

'The procurement system within the public sector is very transparent'.

'The procurement system is still evolving for the public sector but there is room for improving'.

Generally, there is an 'average perception' as it relates to the level of corruption within the public sector but a low perception of corruption within the private sector: 40 per cent of interviewees/ stakeholders rated corruption in the public sector at 6, whereas 50 per cent of interviewees/ stakeholders' rated corruption in the private sector at 4 (see Table 3). It is important to note that Table 3 excludes the perception of members of the media.

Triangulating the comments and the perception data present what can be called an 'uncertain corruption environment', or one in which there is less confidence among individuals to engage in corrupt behaviour. Lambsdorff (2002) argues that confidence in corrupt deals enhances the further spread of corruption. 'When business people have confidence that after paying a bribe a return will be provided as promised, there is less motivation to seek legal alternatives' (ibid.). In the case of Grenada, the uncertain environment is less inviting for public officers to engage in corrupt practices. Lambsdorff's argument and the uncertain corruption environment suggest

Table 3. Perception of corruption within the public and private sectors (scale 1 low – 10 high)

Rating of perception	1	2	3	4	5	6	7	8	9	10
Public sector		20%	20%		20%	40%				
Private sector	25%			50%		25%				

Grenada's CPI score can be partly explained by accepted societal norms, beliefs and values.

The enactment of the procurement legislation demonstrates the Government's commitment to an anti-corruption agenda. Transparency International (2021, p. 21) states that, 'Stronger commitment to procurement reforms and open civic spaces will support greater transparency and accountability'. The procurement process reflects an open, unrestricted, transparent and competitive public call for tenders.

The Fiscal Responsibility Oversight Committee (FROC)

This Committee is responsible, under section 14 (3) of the *Fiscal Responsibility Act* (FRA), for monitoring compliance with the fiscal rules and targets as stipulated in the Act. The FROC is required to report to the House of Representatives annually on the status of implementation of the Act.

Commenting on compliance with fiscal rules and targets in 2019, FROC's most recent Annual Report (2019) states:

> '(a) Government has seen significant improvement in its finances in recent years arising from structural reforms and adjustments. Fiscal prudence, in particular, enhanced tax administration and efficient management of expenditure, needs to be maintained as the economy grows. (b) The FROC continues to hold the view that the Fiscal Authorities now have a firmer handle on the types of debt and a more comprehensive understanding of its dynamics than in the prior years.'

When commenting on outcomes and implications of implementation of the Act, the Report states,

> 'Grenada's fiscal responsibility legislation continued to be implemented amid relatively good economic conditions and the FRA maintained its influence on fiscal policy and fiscal management. The key outcomes and actions in 2019 were (i) year-on year tax collection increases through reinforcement of the compliance strategy; (ii) primary expenditure containment through wage bill restraint and an under-implemented Public Sector Investment Programme (PSIP); and (iii) convergence to the debt target by reducing the total of Central Government debt and guaranteed debt. There were also measures to improve implementation of the PSIP; consultation on impending reforms of the FRA; encouragement for contingency saving; and to commission an independent expenditure review in the public service.'

These comments indicate improved economic/ fiscal management, adherence to established targets and asking the correct questions aimed at problem solving. Such an approach ought to be commended and promoted particularly in an era of uncertainty and rapid change. It is an approach that will promote collaboration, even among contesting ideas, interests and political parties.

Given the objectives of the Act and its responsibilities, the FROC is essentially performing both a monitoring and evaluation function. Monitoring and evaluation are, however, different with respect to their timing and the aspects that they address.

Evaluation is more occasional than monitoring and is typically undertaken 'after the fact', analysing the long-term impact of an intervention. Monitoring, on the other hand, is done periodically during the implementation process. However, what needs to be clearly understood is the linkage and dependencies between planning, monitoring and evaluation (UNEG, 2008). The FROC provides information on strategy (are the right things being done?), operations (are things being done right?) and learning (are there better ways?). The provision of this information promotes accountability and transparency; it can also be seen as a means by which the Government can promote credibility and public confidence in its work and implemented policies. Imas and Rist are of the view that,

> 'Monitoring and evaluation systems are powerful management tools [and] they can help build and foster change in the way governments and organizations operate. They can also help build a knowledge base of what works and what does not.' (2009, p. 34)

Within the context of corruption and good governance, FROC'S work has implications for the media, freedom of information, the engagement of civil society and citizen groups and oversight. Its reports actually empower and strengthen civil society and citizen groups and the media's role in the dissemination of the findings. If there is a case, they can also expose corruption and call for better governance. If there is the need for any of these entities to access FROC'S reports, this can be facilitated through the *Freedom of Information Act, 2007*.

5. Organisational Collaboration, the Media and Civil Society

5.1 Organisational collaboration

The work of the Grenada Integrity Commission (GIC) cannot be accomplished in a vacuum and as such it has surrounded itself with allies who work with it in monitoring, uncovering, educating and mitigating all aspects/reports of corruption in public bodies. This body of stakeholders is called the Integrity Commission Round Table (see Figure 1). Interestingly, the stakeholders' map does not identify the private sector as a stakeholder. Within this context, it is important to note that Act No. 15 of 2007 is 'an Act to make provision for the prevention of corrupt practices by public officers in the performance of public functions, to give effect to the provisions of the OAS Inter-American Convention Against Corruption and for matters connected thereto and for purposes connected therewith'. This wording suggests the focus of the Integrity Commission and its remit is on public officials and not private officials; however, it should be noted that at the practical and operational levels the GIC does engage with the private sector.

As part of its advocacy work, the GIC has identified its key stakeholders and under the auspices of the Commonwealth Secretariat launched its National Roundtable Anti-Corruption Mechanism. The Roundtable facilitates an annual National Roundtable on Anti-Corruption, which involves all the key stakeholders from public sector, private sector, Civil society and the media. In addition, the GIC has sensitised the nation to International Anti-Corruption Day, which is now celebrated annually with the hosting of discussions and seminars/lectures in which one of the main target

Figure 1. Stakeholders

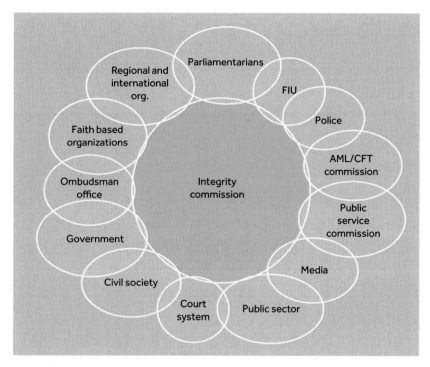

Source: Grenada Integrity Commission website.

groups is schoolchildren. This is a collaborative multi-organizational effort involving a multiplicity of stakeholders such as the FIU, the Audit Department and members of the private sector.

The GIC has a strong public education and advocacy programme with a special focus on young people, recognising that change begins with education. The OECD (2018) argues that building a culture of integrity in society necessarily begins with the education of young people. The knowledge, skills and behaviours they acquire now will shape their country's future and will help them uphold public integrity, which is essential for preventing corruption. Through its programmes, the GIC uses the school systems to raise young people's awareness of the benefits of public integrity. Education for public integrity is about inspiring ethical behaviour and equipping young people with knowledge and skills to resist corruption. This is important because many of these young people will soon be entering the workplace. Such awareness and sensitisation can assist with the creation of 'positive circles' where, according to the theory on the dynamics of corruption, a small reduction of the general corruption level may result in a significant improvement of the situation. They can also help to maintain a low corruption-equilibrium in which both demand and supply are low.

Stakeholder engagement is critical since buy-in from core stakeholders is necessary if education for public integrity is to be effective. Without their support, the programme will not be successful. To facilitate the needed engagement, the GIC has a working group of key stakeholders, including representatives from the ministry of education, the wider public service, security service, religious groups and CSOs. This wide group of stakeholders is effectively a 'network of anti-corruption champions' that strengthens public support for and engagement in anti-corruption efforts. The existence of this network also creates positive circles.

To ensure sustained implementation, monitoring and evaluation during the ongoing COVID-19 pandemic state of emergency, the GIC pivoted to the amplified use of its online presence and e-platforms to ensure the maintenance of its external interface. Administering the survey monkey tool during 2020 and 2021 to national public bodies enabled the completion of the GIC's assessment of the compliance status of public bodies with required legislative and international best practices.

5.2 The media and civil society

The Caribbean is known for a free press and freedom of speech. It is fair to say this statement applies to the media in Grenada. Storr (2016 p. 74) states that,

> 'Given the country's size … there is a lot of media in Grenada. While there is no daily offline newspaper, there are five weekly newspapers, eleven radio stations, three television stations, and one cable provider. Grenada's newspapers are also operating online versions with daily reports" Stoor (2006 p. 74) further goes on to state, "political partisanship is evident in Grenada's media and its history is intertwined with the history of the 1979 revolution". Political partisanship is still evident today in Grenada's newspapers and broadcast media.

The island's media plays a very active role in the fight against corruption by way of advocacy and sensitization. One reporter stated that, 'outcry from the opposition and the media has forced the Government to implement certain pieces of legislation in the fight against corruption'. Similar sentiments were expressed by other interviewees. To give another example, the GIC declaration process requires a declarant to file on the date and time given by the Commission, and extensions of time may be given in approved situations. In 2018 the GIC held six filing of declaration sessions in accordance with its mandate and compliance process. Eight declarants had to be published in the Gazette and in the local newspapers for failure to compile and file their declarations. In so doing, the media is promoting openness of the declaration system and accountability among declarants.

In another case, on the basis of newspaper reports and in keeping with the Commission's mandate, the GIC commenced an investigation into the affairs of a Statutory Authority in August 2018 and took the matter to court. That was the first time that it had undertaken an inquiry of such magnitude and it won. With reference to the role of the media in the fight against corruption in Grenada, the Court's ruling is very interesting. It states that,

> 'I conclude that the media reports concerning the claimant were sufficient – in the words of Wood CJ – to set the Commission's investigative machinery into gear, once the Commission was satisfied that the conduct may be considered dishonest or conducive to corruption.' (paragraph [44])

The outcome of the case will certainly establish a precedent for management of Statutory Bodies and send a message that undertaking corrupt acts can be risky. The case is likely to disturb any corrupt relationships that may exist within the Statutory Body and, in small, close-knit societies such as Grenada, such a disturbance can be profound with far-reaching positive effects.

The outcome of this case, and the recognition of the key role of the media, will certainly encourage members of the media to pay more attention to similar cases. Additionally, the GIC need to get comfortable working with the different sectors of society – civil society and wider public service together with business – because the issues to be addressed have such magnitude that no single entity can solve them on its own. Creation of these partnerships that might be a bit uncomfortable at times but is the only way to drive the systemic changes needed to promote an anti-corruption agenda.

Interestingly, members of the media have a much higher perception of corruption in the public sector the other interviewees, although their perception of corruption in the private sector was similar. On average they rated the public sector at 8 and the private sector at 4. One media interviewee stated that, 'procurement is shrouded, you never know how do you get from project proposal to contract execution, what made one bid successful over the other'. Their attitude may stem from the fact that in the election campaign for the 2008 general election the media accused the then Government and its party, the New National Party (NNP), of corruption and lack of transparency. The National Democratic Congress (NDC) was in office from 2008 to 2013, but when the NNP then returned to power, the media's position towards the party and its government continued. One interviewee stated that, 'even though the government has changed and corruption has reduced, the media continues with the same rhetoric; the narrative has not changed'.

Whatever the reason for the varying views, it can be argued the media's 'corruption-centric' posture has its benefits for the island. Constantly accusing the Government of corruption has the potential:

- To create an uncertain corruption environment;

- To sensitise the wider population and the opposition about corruption, thereby acting as a buffer against any corrupt activity by the Government; and

- To make the Government concerned about corruption and less likely to engage in such.

In essence, the media's actions and utterances has the potential to generate cycles of positive impact in the fight against corruption.

6. International/Regional Organisations

6.1 Integration into regional and international frameworks

In an effort to address the reputational damage that the island suffered during the banking fiasco, Grenada opened itself to global scrutiny so as to align its institutions and laws to that of acceptable regional and international standards. Mainly through the GIC, it has forged alliances, signed on to international conventions and treaties and participated in regional and international forums as it attempts to address corruption and promote good governance. For example, Grenada became a signatory to the Inter American Convention Against Corruption (IACAC) on 15 January, 2002. As a result, the Commission must adhere to the provisions of that Convention and participate in all relevant follow-up mechanisms for giving it effect. The country also acceded to the United Nations Convention Against Corruption (UNCAC) on 1 April 2015, and the Commission must also adhere to the provisions of that Convention and the relevant follow-up mechanisms.

In this context, The Committee of Experts of the Follow-up Mechanism for the Implementation of the IACAC (MESICIC) held an 'on-site' visit to Grenada from 22–24 April 2014 as part of the analysis that the mechanism carries out in accordance with the methodology adopted by consensus among its member countries. MESICIC is a cooperation mechanism between states, with the participation of CSOs, established within the framework of the OAS, in which the legal/institutional framework of each country is reviewed for suitability with the Convention as well as the objective results achieved. The results of this visit form part of the review process that is carried out by the Committee of Experts.

During the visit, the representatives of MESICIC gathered information on the implementation in Grenada of the provision of the IACAC regarding oversight bodies, specifically the Audit Department, the Office of the Director of Public Prosecutions, the Public Service Commission, and the GIC. MESICIC made certain recommendations aimed at strengthening and improving the functions of the oversight bodies. In the case of the GIC (referred to as the IC), it recommended that it,

> 'specify its functions vis-à-vis those of the PSC with respect to disciplinary oversight of public servants; adopt a Code of Conduct and other regulations provided for under the Integrity in Public Life Act; determine the scope of the IC's role in reviewing asset disclosure statements; adopt coordination and support mechanisms with other bodies; implement a merit based selection system, a disciplinary system, and a training plan for its staff; post a copy of its annual activities report and information on its mission, tasks, and activities on the government's website; ensure timely delivery of the resources the IC needs to discharge its functions; adopt a follow-up mechanism that enables the IC to ascertain the outcomes of investigations into cases of wrongdoing brought to the attention of the competent authorities; and develop statistical data on the results of its work in order to identify challenges and recommend, where appropriate, corrective measures.' (MESICIC, 2014, p. i)

Also, in the case of the Director of Public Prosecutions it recommended that it,

> 'adopt the measures necessary to preserve its operational autonomy; adopt coordination measures with other bodies; ensure the timely delivery of the budget resources the DPP needs to discharge its functions; assign a sufficient number of

prosecutors and support staff to it and ensure that prosecutors receive periodic training on how to prosecute corrupt acts; implement a system of follow-up for the cases of corruption the DPP initiates that enables it to find out how such cases are proceeding and what the outcomes are; develop and publish statistical data that makes it possible to ascertain clearly which of the cases prosecuted by the DPP are specifically related to corrupt acts as well as the outcomes of such cases, in order to identify challenges and recommend, where appropriate, corrective measures; and disseminate, via the government's website, information on the DPP's activities, challenges, and the results of its prosecution of corrupt acts.' (MESICIC, 2014, p. ii)

They also obtained information on the implementation of the recommendations that were formulated by the MESICIC to Grenada in the first round, pertaining, among others, to the prevention of conflicts of interest, preservation of public resources and civil society participation. Members of the Commission also had the opportunity to meet with civil society and private sector organizations to address issues related to cooperation between them and public institutions in the fight against corruption, citizen participation mechanisms and access to public information as well as any difficulties faced in the implementation of such recommendations (OAS, 2004).

The Government had to respond, as best as it could, to these and other recommendations from MESICIC. Working to implement the recommendations whilst establishing the corresponding institutional relationships, which is essentially an accreditation process, has the potential to unleash a virtuous circle reinforcing the aims and objectives of MESICIC. Such reinforcement has positive feedback effects that over time would significantly assist in institutionalizing the fight against corruption. The net effect of this accreditation process and its related guidelines/ standards create an environment that is less facilitatory to corruption and all its negative effects, particularly within a small state. Essentially the positive feedback here is driven by external conditions/forces.

In addition, Grenada has a mechanism in place for the exchange of information with the United States and it has therefore established laws and regulations ensuring the availability to US and other foreign government's personnel of adequate records in connection with drug investigations and proceedings. Drug trafficking, fraud and under-invoicing are identifiable avenues for money laundering in Grenada.

6.2 Collaboration with the World Bank and the Commonwealth Secretariat

The GIC has also collaborated with the World Bank in the area of National Risk Assessment. The World Bank National Money Laundering Risk Assessment Tool has been developed to identify and assess the real sources of money laundering and terrorist financing risks in a jurisdiction. The World Bank has partnered with the FIU in this exercise and, on their recommendation, the FIU invited the Integrity Commission and other stakeholders to be part of the establishment of a National Risk Assessment Working Group, to identify risks related to money laundering and terrorist financing in the country. The Working Group was divided into teams, with each team having responsibility for one of the nine modules that make up this tool. The work was undertaken in three phases: the preparation phase; the assessment and collection of data phase; and the final phase, which consisted of the review of the risk assessment results and design of risk-based action plans.

In order to fulfil its mandate, the GIC is fully aware of the need to equip its employees and stakeholders with the requisite skills and competencies. It sought technical support from the Commonwealth Secretariat to facilitate training for the Commission and its other major stakeholders. The request for assistance from the Chairman specifically asked the Secretariat, 'to organise anti-corruption programmes for the Integrity Commission and other law enforcement agencies in Grenada'. Against this background the Secretariat designed and delivered a programme targeting senior and middle level management officials of anti-corruption agencies including the Office of the Integrity Commission, Ombudsman, Audit Department, Department of Public Administration (DPA), Revenue Collection Agencies, Enforcement Agencies and Statutory Authorities.

The purpose and specific objectives of that programme were as follows:

- To provide positive anti-corruption measures for implementation by the Integrity Commission to reduce or prevent corruption and improve good governance; and

- To expose participants to measurements and frameworks for fighting corruption.

Through these interventions, participants gained a deeper understanding of anti-corruption frameworks and strategies that can be adapted and applied to combat corruption in the country. Their technical know-how and skills in corruption control were strengthened and they learnt how to better manage corruption risks. Grenada is the regional Centre for Excellence in collaboration with the Commonwealth Secretariat to facilitate and foster national and regional cross fertilisation and strategies on anti-corruption.

In summary, the Grenadian Government through the GIC has networked and collaborated internationally and regionally in the fight against corruption by way of capacity-building initiatives, sharing of critical information, being signatory to treaties and advocating for the anti- corruption cause. Grenada is also a member of the Commonwealth Caribbean Association of Integrity Commissions and Anti-Corruption Bodies (CCAICACB). The key objectives of the CCAICACB are to afford member states/organisations the opportunity to share information on operations and best practices in the anti-corruption fight and the identification and prevention of corrupt activities. Additionally, it provides an environment for networking and collaboration and assists member states/organisations to establish and standardise necessary legal frameworks. The Chairman of the GIC was once the Chairman of the CCAICACB Executive. By way of all these initiatives Grenada has built organisational structures, strengthened its human resource capabilities, built international networks and inserted itself into the international and regional frameworks aimed at fighting corruption. This approach certainly has the potential to assist any country in its fight against corruption.

7. Conclusions: Challenges, Lessons and Recommendations

The enactment of the plethora of legislation, alignment of its institutions and laws to that of acceptable regional and international standards, establishment of anti-corruption agencies and building of international and regional anti-corruption networks by the Government were all aimed at addressing corruption. The approach taken is 'fix the system, not the politicians'. For as long as politics is seen as a war between good and bad individuals while ignoring the structures that reward or punish them, corruption will continue. Warped systems enable political corruption because systems drive behaviour. Bad politicians are not necessarily bad people, but often society implicitly or explicitly encourages their behaviour. Corruption creates economic inefficiencies and inequities, but reforms are possible to reduce the material benefits from payoffs. Corruption is not just an economic problem; it is also intertwined with politics. Reform may require changes in both constitutional structures and the underlying relationship of the market and the state. Effective reform cannot occur unless both the international community and domestic political leaders support change.

Factors such as political commitment, social trust towards government institutions and historical institutional traditions, among others, are important to the effectiveness of anti-corruption initiatives. One ought to be mindful about the context since a multiplicity of factors affecting national anti-corruption dynamics make it difficult to determine how much of the success can be assigned to any factor. In this sense, Acemoglu and Robinson (2012) argue that the differences in development among former British colonies is explained by the type of institutional configurations: those countries under inclusive institutions enjoy prosperity and sustainable development, whereas those countries under extractive institutions cannot bring about sustainable growth. These realities need to be remembered when focusing on challenges, lessons and recommendations.

7.1 Challenges

The size, geographic location and stage of development of Small Island Developing States (SIDS), such as those in the Caribbean, mean that these countries literally cannot afford to tolerate acts of corruption. In small islands, decisions in the economic, political and legal fields have a pervasiveness that they lack in large societies. Benedict (1967) contends that this is because people are connected to each other in many different ways in small societies; and in such societies one cannot progress very far occupationally or professionally without coming into contact with the government. Many roles are played by a few individuals so the same individuals constantly interact. Benedict's position on the impact of smallness is reflected in comments from a senior public officer, who stated that, 'the society is small so people know each other. There are times when someone will ask you as a public officer to do them a favour and they may offer you something for helping them. Is that corruption? These people do not see such as corruption, so they do it without any sense of guilt'.

This has profound implications for economic and social development since decisions and choices of individuals will be influenced by their relations in many contexts with other individuals. This reality creates an environment where reporting acts of corruption may be challenging because of the possibility of being targeted and labelled as an informer. This situation serves to reinforce the reluctance to be a whistle-blower and as such has left room for corruption to grow in the Caribbean, even in the face of improvements in legislation and oversight institutions.

7.2 Lessons

Based on the review the following are some of the key lessons learnt:

- An ongoing national corruption crisis has the potential to act as a trigger for reform, leading to a reduction of corruption and to good governance;

- With strong political will, a country with a high level of corruption can be transformed to a low corruption country;

- A well-functioning anti-corruption framework is dependent on whole-of- government cross-organisational collaboration and a high degree of professionalism among the responsible public officials;

- The enactment of appropriate legislation is central in the fight against corruption and the promotion of good governance;

- Anti-corruption agencies and key stakeholder organisations working collaboratively has the potential to promote learnings that can then lead to improvements in the systems and processes that are used in the fight against corruption;

- International collaboration has the potential to strengthen domestic anti-corruption initiatives and improve outcomes;

- Access to information should be a number one rule in procurement procedures; and

- Technical expertise among public officials is important for an effective and efficient procurement system.

7.3 Recommendations

It can be argued that the small and close-knit nature of societies such as Grenada means they are very prone to corruption and abuse of political power and, therefore, need even more oversight with stronger processes and systems of control for their effective and efficient management. Against this background, the following recommendations are made:

- The internal regulatory mechanisms of government – accounting and audit, procurement and personnel – should be the centrepiece of reforms to promote accountability and good governance;

- There should be paperless declaration so as to facilitate storage and higher compliance;

- There should be rotation of public officials responsible for procurement within a certain area;

- There should be stricter enforcement of anti-corruption legislation;

- There is the need to increase sensitisation of the public in the use of the newly simplified systems to encourage reporting cases of corruption;

- There should be the promotion of open access to information;

- There should be harmonising of the procurement processes at the OECS level, along with transparent cross-regional procurement, particularly of expensive and high-value items. This is particularly so with goods and services that require a service contract over time and where significant value can be sought with a collective approach;

- There should be increased use of ICTs, both in the tendering process to achieve greater transparency and competitiveness, and also in generating effective real-time inventories of existing plant, expertise and procurement plans.

Finally, the findings on Grenada with its 'uncertain corruption environment' have much to teach the Caribbean as it grapples with the challenges of corruption and the promotion of good governance.

Bibliography

Print and online publications

Acemoglu, D and J Robinson (2012) *Why Nations Fail: The Origins of Power, Prosperity, and Poverty*. New York: Crown Publishing Group.

Andvig, J and K Moene (1990) 'How Corruption May Corrupt'. *Journal of Economic Behaviour and Organization* 13(1): 63–76.

Benedict, B (ed.) (1967) *Problems of Smaller Territories*. London: Athlone Press for the Institute of Commonwealth Studies.

Caribbean Financial Action Task Force (2014) 'Ninth Follow Up Report'. St. George's, Grenada.

Edwards, v. Grenada Integrity Commission. GDAHCV 2019/0038 (Eastern Caribbean Supreme Court of Grenada).

Fiscal Responsibility Oversight Committee, (2018). 2017 Annual Report. St. George's: Government of Grenada.

Fiscal Responsibility Oversight Committee, (2019). 2018 Annual Report. St. George's: Government of Grenada.

Grenade, WC (2012) 'Governance in the Caribbean: Challenges and Prospects'. In: Robertson, and R Jones-Parry (eds.), *Commonwealth Governance Handbook 2012/13: Democracy, Development and Public Administration*, 54–57. Cambridge: Nexus Strategic Partnership.

Imas, L. and R Rist (2009) *The Road to Results: Designing and Conducting Effective Development Evaluations*. Washington, DC: The World Bank.

James, R et al. (2019) 'Explaining High Unemployment in ECCU Countries'. IMF Working Paper WP/19/144. Washington, DC: International Monetary Fund

Kirton, M (2011) Feasibility Study on the Establishment of a Public Service Training Institute in Grenada

Lambsdorff, J (2002) 'Making Corrupt Deals: Contracting in the Shadow of the Law'. *Journal of Economic Behaviour and Organization* 48: 221–241.

OAS (Organization of American States) (2014a) 'OAS Anticorruption Mechanism Holds On-Site Visit to Grenada'. Press release, 9 April. https://www.oas.org/en/media_center/press_release.asp?sCodigo=E-141/14

OAS (Organization of American States) (2014b) 'Mechanism for the Follow-up on the Implementation of the Inter-American Convention against Corruption'. Twenty-Fourth Meeting of the Committee of Experts, Washington, DC.

OECD (Organisation for Economic Co-operation and Development) (2017) *Effective Inter-Agency Co-operation in Fighting Tax Crimes and Other Financial Crimes.* Third Edition. Paris: OECD Publishing.

OECD (Organisation for Economic Co-operation and Development) (2018) *Education for Integrity Teaching on Anti-Corruption, Values and the Rule of Law.* Paris: OECD Publishing.

OECD (Organisation for Economic Co-operation and Development) (2021) *Ending the Shell Game: Cracking Down on the Professionals Who Enable Tax and White Collar Crimes.* Paris: OECD Publishing.

Office of the Integrity Commission (2017) 'Fourth Annual Report'. St George, Grenada.

Office of the Integrity Commission (2018) 'Fifth Annual Report'. St George, Grenada.

Office of the Integrity Commission (2019) 'Sixth Annual Report'. St George, Grenada.

Office of the Integrity Commission, Declarations Received by the Commission 2014-2021.

Office of the Integrity Commission (Undated) 'Profile of the Integrity Commission'. St. George, Grenada.

Søreide, T (2002) 'Corruption in Public Procurement: Causes, Consequences and Cures'. CMI Report. Bergen, Norway: Chr. Michelsen Institute.

Storr, J (2016) *Journalism in a Small Place: Making Caribbean News Relevant, Comprehensive, and Independent.* Calgary: University of Calgary Press.

Tanzi, V (1998) 'Corruption and the Budget: Problems and Solutions'. In: Jain, KA (ed.) *Economics of Corruption.* London: Kluwer Academic Publishers.

Transparency International (2017). Corruption Perception Index 2016, Berlin: Transparency International.

Transparency International (2018). Corruption Perception Index 2017, Berlin: Transparency International.

Transparency International (2019). Corruption Perception Index 2018, Berlin: Transparency International.

Transparency International (2020). Corruption Perception Index 2019, Berlin: Transparency International.

Transparency International (2021). Corruption Perception Index 2020, Berlin: Transparency International.

Transparency International (2022) 'What Is Corruption?' https://www.transparency.org/en/what-is-corruption

UNDP (United Nations Development Programme) (1999). 'Fighting Corruption to Improve Governance'. Policy Document. New York: UNDP.

UNEG (United Nations Evaluation Group) (2008) 'UNEG Training: What a UN Evaluator Needs to Know'. Module 1. New York: UNEG.

United Nations Convention against Corruption Grenada-20160512-095237 Assessor: Comments: Grenada 31/08/2016.

Woodard, C (2008) 'Post-Ponzi Scheme, Grenada to Reopen for Offshore Banking'. *The Christian Science Monitor*, 31 May. https://www.csmonitor.com/World/Americas/2008/0531/p12s01-woam.html

Worldometer (2022) 'Population of Grenada (2020 and Historical)'. https://www.worldometers.info/world-population/grenada-population/

World Bank (1997) *World Development Report 1997: The State in a Changing World.* New York: Oxford University Press.

World Bank (2000) *Reforming Public Institutions and Strengthening Governance: A World Bank Strategy.* Washington, DC. The World Bank.

World Bank (2010) *Doing Business 2011: Making a Difference for Entrepreneurs.* Washington, DC: The World Bank.

World Bank (2020) *Doing Business 2020: Comparing Business Regulation in 190 Economies.* Washington, DC: The World Bank.

Legislation

The Grenada Authority for the Regulation of Financial Institutions Act, No.5 of 2006

The Proceeds of Crime Act, No. 16 of 2012

The Prevention of Corruption Act, No. 15 of 2007

The Grenada Authority for the Regulation of Financial Institutions Act, No.1 of 2008

The Terrorism Act No. 16 of 2012

Integrity in Public Life Act No. 24 of 2013

The Public Procurement and Disposal of Public Property Act, No. 39 of 2014

Fiscal Responsibility Act No. 29 of 2015

'The Public Procurement and Disposal of Public Property Regulations, 2015'

Appendix A. Questionnaire

I. INTERNAL STAKEHOLDERS – GRENADA INTEGRITY COMMISSION (GIC)

1. Are you satisfied with the mandate of the Grenada Integrity Commission?

   YES

   NO (give reasons)

2. Are you satisfied with the manner in which the GIG executes its mandate?

   YES

   NO (give reasons)

3. In the fight against corruption what needs to be done in terms of:

    - Assets declaration and compliance

    - Investigations

    - Public sensitisation and education

    - Other/s

4. What was the core strategic focus/objective of the GIC over the last five years?

5. Over that five-year period, how did the GIC work with its key stakeholders to achieve its strategic focus/objectives

6. What evidence exists to demonstrate there is improvement in the work of the GIC since its inception? (Please explain in detail)

7. What are the major constraints faced by the GIC in executing its mandate? (Please explain in detail)

8. Feel free to comment on:

    - Challenges/problems within your context

    - What needs to be done to address corruption in Grenada

    - Your systems and procedures

    - Your stakeholders

    - Institutional needs

II. EXTERNAL STAKEHOLDERS – Grenada Integrity Commission

1. Are you satisfied with the manner in which the GIG executes its mandate?

    YES

    NO (give reasons)

2. In the fight against corruption what needs to be done in terms of:

    - Assets declaration and compliance

    - Investigations

    - Public sensitisation and education

    - Other/s

3. On a scale of 1–10 (with 1 being low and 10 being high), how do you rate the performance of the GIC?

    Comments

4. On a scale of 1–10 (with 1 being low and 10 being high), what is your perception of corruption in the (a) public and (b) private sectors in Grenada?

    Comments

5. Is there any evidence to demonstrate there is improvement in the work of the GIC since its inception? (Please explain in detail)

6. Are you satisfied with the procurement system within the public sector? (Please explain in detail)

7. In you view what are the major cause/s of corruption in Grenada? (Please explain in detail)

8. Fell free to comment on:

    -   Corruption challenges/problems in Grenada

    -   What needs to be done to address corruption in Grenada

    -   Government procurement system

Appendix B. Checklist

1. Views about Transparency International's CPI

2. Grenada ratings over the last 5 years

3. On a scale of 1–10 (with 1 being low and 10 being high), how do you rate the performance of the GIC?

    Comments

4. On a scale of 1–10 (with 1 being low and 10 being high), what is your perception of corruption in the (a) public and (b) private sectors in Grenada?

    Comments

5. Government procurement

6. Grenada private sector

7. Role of the media

8. Comment on:

    -   Corruption challenges/problems in Grenada

    -   What needs to be done to address corruption in Grenada

    -   Behaviour of public officials

Chapter 6

St Lucia

Dawn De Coteau PhD

Abstract

St Lucia has ranked above the world average and scored as one of the top four countries in the Caribbean region in Transparency International's Corruption Perception Index (CPI) for over 10 years. This consistently high score has demonstrated that the country has and continues to make great strides in progressing the anti-corruption agenda across legal and institutional frameworks. This report, therefore, examines the anti-corruption approaches adopted by St Lucia over the years. The methodology applied was a qualitative case study including a desk review and semi-structured interviews. The period of research was eight weeks, from 1 March to 21 May 2021. Overall, it is evident that the country has enacted significant pieces of anti-corruption legislation and established various institutions to support the agenda. However, there remain challenges for St Lucia in sharing these achievements across the sectors to enable all citizens to recognise its journey of travel to date.

1. Introduction

This report seeks to identify the factors that have contributed to St Lucia's success in tackling corruption by analysing both technical and political anti-corruption strategies.

Research on any subject cannot be undertaken in isolation (Aveyard, 2011). A review of the current literature is fundamental. It illustrates what has already been written about the subject matter under research, enabling the researcher to identify gaps and offer new thinking, contribution, and recommendations. Over the last hundred years, much has been written about corruption, and the last half-century has seen interest in the topic gathering momentum. In the past two decades, innovative projects such as Transparency International's Corruption Perception Index (CPI) have been established, and their data have contributed to a wide range of macro- and micro-level studies (Mauro 1995, Johnston, 2005). The literature review is, therefore, a critical element throughout the report.

Following this introduction, the report looks at the methodology adopted and some of the key themes that emerged from the data stemming from the qualitative interviews. It then outlines the relevant anti-corruption indices followed by a definition of corruption in section 3. The fourth section provides an overview of the socio-economic and political environment of St Lucia, while the fifth examines the country's legal and institutional backing for anti-corruption. Section 6 provides an analysis of the data gathered from various stakeholders, including the private sector, civil society and the media as well as international and regional organisations. The seventh section discusses ways in which the Government can engage with stakeholders to prevent corruption. Finally, the conclusion, lessons, challenges and recommendations are presented in section 8.

2. Methodology

The study utilised a qualitative case study research design. A case study as defined by Creswell (2013, p. 97) is,

> '...a qualitative approach in which the investigator explores a bounded system (case)... over time ... involving multiples sources of information and reports a case and case descriptions based on themes.'

Several factors defined the perimeters for this case study in keeping with best practices in conducting such research (Baxter and Jack, 2008). These include the time, activity and place (Miles and Huberman, 1994). This single case study of St Lucia focused on various anti-corruption efforts over the period 2011 to 2021.

Desk review

A review of media reports covering corruption in St Lucia over the period 2011–2021 was conducted. These sources were primarily online articles and editorials, which were used to provide an overview of the critical issues in understanding corruption and key initiatives to combat it. In addition to media reports, other technical documents were reviewed from online sources of government, international organisations and regional organisations that include references to corruption or anti-corruption efforts in St Lucia. In addition, the legislation and institutional frameworks were reviewed.

Interviews

Semi-structured interviews were conducted in two phases: the first in March 2021 and the second in May 2021. Berg (2007) characterised the semi-structured interview as involving a number of predetermined questions and special topics. While questions are typically asked systematically in a consistent order, interviews are allowed to digress, and interviewers are expected to probe far beyond the answers to their prepared standardised questions.

A list of interviewees from across the public, private and civil society sectors was identified and sent an introductory letter from the Commonwealth Secretariat explaining the research study, along with a letter inviting individuals to participate in an interview. A total of 12 persons were invited to participate, and the response rate was seven. Interview questions focused on key themes around corruption such as prevention, criminalisation and sanctions (see the Appendix). All the necessary ethical considerations were adhered to, including anonymity and confidentiality. In addition, as the research focussed on what could be viewed as a sensitive topic regarding cultural norms and values (McCosker, 2001), consideration was given to these factors throughout the interviews. These were conducted via phone and Zoom and lasted for one hour. In most instances, respondents requested to remain anonymous.

Figure 1. Key themes in the study

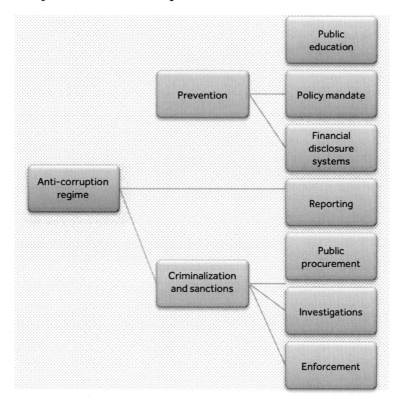

Data analysis

As noted earlier, case studies synthesise data gathered from multiple sources organised into key themes. Figure 1 illustrates the key themes covered in the study. The primary and secondary themes are in yellow and green, respectively. Those themes were adapted from the general literature on anti-corruption, while the tertiary themes outlined in blue were gleaned from the interviews conducted and other documents researched.

3. Anti-Corruption Indices and Definition of Corruption

3.1 St Lucia's ranking on anti-corruption indices

St Lucia has been assessed by various global ratings as to its ability to combat corruption. Two of the most prominent indicators are Transparency International's Corruption Perceptions Index (CPI) and the World Bank Good Governance Indicators.

Figure 2 shows the CPI ratings for the Commonwealth Caribbean over the period 2012–2020. In all instances, St Lucia scored in the top four countries in the Caribbean region (and was also above the world average, which was less than 50). While scores ranged from a low of 55 (over the past two years) to a high of 71 (the first three years), St Lucia scored higher than the two most developed Commonwealth Caribbean

Figure 2. Commonwealth Caribbean CPI score, 2012–2020

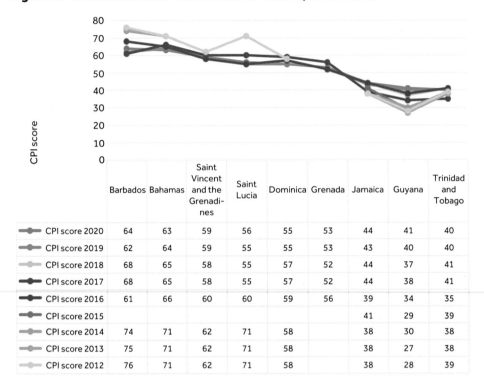

	Barbados	Bahamas	Saint Vincent and the Grenadines	Saint Lucia	Dominica	Grenada	Jamaica	Guyana	Trinidad and Tobago
CPI score 2020	64	63	59	56	55	53	44	41	40
CPI score 2019	62	64	59	55	55	53	43	40	40
CPI score 2018	68	65	58	55	57	52	44	37	41
CPI score 2017	68	65	58	55	57	52	44	38	41
CPI score 2016	61	66	60	60	59	56	39	34	35
CPI score 2015							41	29	39
CPI score 2014	74	71	62	71	58		38	30	38
CPI score 2013	75	71	62	71	58		38	27	38
CPI score 2012	76	71	62	71	58		38	28	39

Source: Transparency International, 2021.

countries (Jamaica and Trinidad and Tobago), which scored below 50 in all instances. In other words, when compared to other Commonwealth Caribbean countries, St Lucia is seen as a less corrupt or cleaner country.

Figure 3 illustrates the corruption ranking of Commonwealth Caribbean countries on the World Governance Indicators (WGI) for 2012–2019. Percentile rank 0 to 100 indicates the rank of the country among all countries in the world, with 0 corresponding to the lowest rank and 100 corresponding to the highest. Here we see that St Lucia has been ranked in the high 60s to low 80s over this period, with the highest rank being 81.04 in 2012, followed by 81.52 in 2013. The lowest-ranked positions for St Lucia were 67.31 in 2014 and 69.23 in 2019, respectively. When comparing the ranks of other Commonwealth Caribbean countries, St Lucia is one of the higher-ranked countries along with Antigua and Barbuda, The Bahamas, Barbados and St Vincent and the Grenadines. The Commonwealth Caribbean countries with the lowest ranks are Dominica, Jamaica and St Kitts.

Anti-corruption initiatives are viewed as good governance arrangements. Andersson and Heywood (2009, p. 747) describe good governance as 'improving political accountability, strengthening civil society, promoting competition via markets and the private sector, imposing institutional restraints on power and reforming public sector management'.

Figure 3. Control of corruption in the Commonwealth Caribbean, percentile rank, 2012–2019

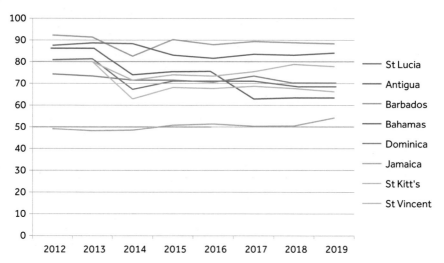

Source: World Bank, 2021.

3.2 Defining corruption

There is no universal definition of corruption; however, Nye (1967), Heidenheimer (1978) and Johnston (2005) viewed it as the abuse of public power for personal gain, through bribery, where illegal payment is made to a government official in return for a governmental or state-sanctioned act that requires some form of selective process. Akindele (1995) defines corruption as forms of reciprocal behaviour or transaction where holders of power and office can use rewards to induce each other to grant preferential treatment or favour, against the principles and interest of other organisations within the society. These definitions and understandings of corrupt behaviour have been accepted by international organisations and others, including CARICOM, the European Union (EU) and the World Bank, which agree that corruption is, therefore, an abuse of entrusted power for personal gain or for the benefit of a group to which one owes allegiance, which is the definition adopted in this study.

4. Political and Socio-Economic Context

St Lucia is a Commonwealth country located in the Caribbean Sea with a total landmass of 616 square kilometres. The island was formed by volcanic activity, and its geographic features include mountains, rivers and boiling sulphur springs (Commonwealth Secretariat, 2021). It has a history of European colonial rule, with contested possession between England and France throughout the 17th and 18th centuries, where it changed rulers 14 times and was finally conceded to the United Kingdom in 1814.

The population of 182,790 is fairly evenly split between the rural and urban areas, with the highest number living in the capital, Castries. The population is mainly of African or mixed African-European descent, with Afro-Caribbeans accounting for 68 per cent, mixed 17 per cent, Europeans 5 per cent and Indo-Caribbeans 3 per cent (World Population Review, 2021).

The official language is English; however, 95 per cent of the population speak French Creole (Patwah). In terms of religion, 70 per cent of the population are Catholics, with the remainder belonging to various other religious denominations, including Seventh Day Adventist and Pentecostal (World Population Review, 2021).

4.1 Politics

St Lucia obtained independence from the British Empire in 1979 and adopted the Westminster model of governance. It continues to maintain its status as a Constitutional Monarchy, with the Crown represented as the Head of State by the Governor General. It is a stable parliamentary democracy with free, fair and competitive elections and a long experience of peaceful transfer of power between rival parties (Freedom House, 2021). As a bicameral system, it has two chambers in the legislature: the House of Representatives and the Senate. Members of the former are elected to one of 17 seats. In the Senate, six members are appointed on the recommendation of the Prime Minister, three on the nomination of the leader of the opposition and two are directly appointed by the Governor General.

The country follows the Westminster tradition of government where the Prime Minister is Head of Government while the Governor General is Head of State. The Prime Minister is elected and is the head of the majority party in the legislature. The cabinet comprises the Prime Minister, Attorney General and Ministers. St Lucia's legal system is based primarily on British Common law, with its civil codes and laws pertaining to property influenced by French law. All three arms of government (executive, legislative, judicial) work closely to achieve the overall governance of the country.

4.2 The economy

St Lucia has been able to attract foreign business and investment, especially in relation to both offshore banking and tourism industries. The economy is predominantly dependent on income from tourism, which accounts for 65 per cent of gross domestic product (GDP) and is its main source of foreign exchange earnings. Like most Eastern Caribbean islands, it continues to produce bananas, mangoes and avocados for export; however, the competitive edge that it once held has been removed as a result of strong competition (Moody's Analytics, 2021).

St Lucia is vulnerable to a number of factors, including external shocks, volatile tourism receipts, natural disasters and dependence on foreign oil. This, coupled with the high public debt (in the region of 77 per cent of GDP in 2012) and high debt servicing obligations makes it difficult for the country to respond to adverse external shocks (ibid.).

4.3 Education

St Lucia's education system is similar to the British system. The *Education Act (1997)* provides for all students to attend school until they reach 16 years, whilst the *Universal Secondary School Act (2006)* guarantees every student a secondary school place to complete their five-year basic studies from form 1 to 5. For the small percentage of children who do not fit into the traditional educational system, a three-year Senior Programme or CARE School is offered, which is comparable to a vocational educational programme and focuses on preparing students for future employment.

5. Legal and Institutional Backing for Anti-corruption

St Lucia has enacted/established a raft of legal and primary institutional frameworks to assist in combating corruption. It has signed and ratified both the United Nations Convention against Corruption (UNCAC) and the Inter-American Convention against Corruption (IACAC). Both conventions provide for various legislative and policy measures that the Government should adopt to prevent and combat corruption.

5.1 Legal system

In terms of domestic anti-corruption laws, St Lucia has enshrined in its Constitution the establishment of the Integrity Commission and has enacted since 2004 the *Integrity in Public Life Act*, which covers financial disclosure for persons in public life, declaration of receipts of gifts and specific corruption acts. The penalty for any public servant failing to meet the deadline to declare is a fine of up to the US$50,000.00 or up to five years in prison.

The St Lucia Constitution Order No.12 of 1978 and the *Audit Act No.26 of 1988* establish the Office of the Director of Audit and for the Director of Audit to assist Parliament in holding the Government accountable. The crucial piece of legislation is section 7 of the *Audit Act*, which provides for the Director of Audit to scrutinise the accounts of St Lucia, including those relating to consolidated funds, public bodies, statutory bodies and government companies.

In addition, St Lucia has enacted *The Procurement and Asset Disposal Act (2015)*, the objective of which is to strengthen the procurement procedures in key respects, providing guarantees that tendering processes are open. It also provides mechanisms to ensure that the government agents who procure do not have conflicts of interest.

With respect to government transparency, St Lucia has drafted the *Freedom of Information Act (2009)*, which guarantees access to information upon request. It is important to note in the Bill prescribes that access to information can only be denied in cases of national security.

In addition to the above, St Lucia has enacted new laws and amended several pieces of legislation that are relevant in assisting the country to meaningfully address anti-corruption. These include:

- The *Financial Services Regulatory Authority Act No.13 2011* (FSRAA) was established to regulate providers of financial services and provide for other related financial matters. The FSRAA has a key role in terms of transparency, which is placed at the centre of its mission statement, 'to maintain the integrity of the financial sector through the efficient and effective administration of the laws and regulations, application of the best international standards and practices, and effective supervision of registered entities operating in the sector' (FSRAA, 2021).

- The *Money Laundering (Prevention) Act No 8 of 2010* (MLPA) and the *Money Service Business Act No.11 of 2010* (MSBA), which were enacted to provide for the licensing and regulation of money services businesses and to make provision for related matters. These two pieces of legislation will assist financial institutions in detecting and combating money laundering and preventing criminals from undertaking illegal transactions through which they frequently disguise the origins of their funds connected to illegal activity.

- The *Proceeds of Crime Act* (POCA) was amended through the *Proceeds of Crime (Amendment) Act No.4 of 2010* and the *Proceeds of Crime (Amendment) Act No.15 of 2011*, which allow for forfeiture and confiscation orders to be given in addition to a sentence with a view to ensuring the guilty person is deprived of the benefits from the crime.

In May 2010, the Money Laundering (Prevention)(Guidance Notes) Regulation was made by the then Attorney General pursuant to section 43 of the 2010 MLPA incorporating the guidelines made by the FIA. This was followed by the Money Laundering (Prevention) (Guidelines for Other Business Activity) Regulations as Statutory Instrument 2012, No. 83, and the Amendments to the Money Laundering (Prevention) (Guidance Notes) (Amendment) Regulations as Statutory Instrument 2012 No. 82 were brought into force in August 2012. Both pieces of legislation were further strengthened with a view to progressing efforts to fight corruption through monitoring and supervising roles.

Additionally, St Lucia has implemented a code of conduct and regulation for non-profit organisations to promote transparency and accountability.

Also to be noted is that St Lucia acceded to the UN Convention for the Suppression of the Financing of Terrorism and the UN Convention against Corruption on 18 November and 25 November 2011, respectively. It also signed an MOU with St Vincent and the Grenadines.

5.2 Institutional framework

St Lucia has several institutions that are assisting in the anti-corruption agenda. As well as operating as regulatory institutions, these organisations also undertake stakeholder engagement. Both internal and external stakeholders have a role to play in the anti- corruption agenda. According to Hanson (2011), external stakeholders, including citizens users, professional and business organisations, have become more interested in the management of corruption risk. However, (Monteduro et al., 2021) argue internal stakeholders, including employees and governing bodies, also have a role to play in managing corruption risks.

Financial Intelligence Authority (FIA)

The FIA was established in 2003 pursuant to the provisions of the *Financial Intelligence Authority Act 2002* and through the *Money Laundering (Prevention) Act 12.20 of 2013* Revised Law of St Lucia (MLPA).

The FIA has several key responsibilities, including receiving, analysing, obtaining, investigating and disseminating information that relates to the proceeds of criminal acts and, in particular, information derived from suspicious transaction reports. Its mandate is detecting, preventing and prosecuting money laundering and other serious crimes as well as confiscating the proceeds of crime (Financial Intelligence Authority, 2021). In addition, the FIA has supervision, monitoring, international cooperation and advisory remits.

Office of Director of Audit (ODA)

The ODA was established by the St Lucia Constitution Order No.12 of 1978 and the *Audit Act No 26 of 1988*. The office is constitutional and reports to the House of Parliament through the Ministry of Finance but is independent of government. Reports that set out audit findings are produced annually. The mission statement of the Director of Audit is,

> 'To promote greater accountability in the public service through a professional approach to monitoring and reporting on whether monies appropriated by Parliament were applied as appropriated; whether expenditure conforms to the authority that governs it on the efficiency, economy and effectiveness of government spending.' (Office of the Director of Audit, 2021)

The Integrity Commission

The Integrity Commission was established through the *Integrity in Public Life Act No. 6 of 2004*, which gives it authority to supervise, monitor and sanction persons in public life. It is the main anti-corruption body and therefore its work and performance is of paramount importance to achieving good governance and combating corruption in St Lucia. A key function of the Commission is the Declaration of Assets, in which the Commission obtains written declarations of Senators and Members of Parliament (MPs) and others as Parliament prescribes pertaining to their assets, liabilities and income (Constitution of St Lucia, 2021). Any prescribed person failing to comply is subject to being publicly reported.

Office of Private Sector Relations (OPSR)

The OPSR sits within the Ministry of Commerce, Enterprise, Development and Consumer Affairs, and its main objectives are to stimulate and promote business growth and development across the economy. This is achieved with an emphasis on creating and sustaining a strong business environment, facilitating the development of human resource capabilities, providing support for enhancing business competitiveness and facilitating capacity building in various areas including anti-corruption.

The Financial Services Regulatory Authority (FSRA)

The FSRA is the regulatory body that licenses, supervises and regulates the operations of the financial sector. It assumed all responsibility of the Financial Sector Supervision Unit (FSSU) and the credit union supervision function of the Department of Co-operatives within the Ministry of Finance. Additionally, it regulates the Saint Lucia Development Bank (SLDB). The FSRA's mission is to maintain the integrity of the financial sector through the efficient and effective administration of laws and regulations, application of best international standards and practices and effective supervision of registered entities operating in the sector.

The Saint Lucia Police Force (SLPF)

The SLPF was established in 1834 and is responsible for law enforcement. It oversees the FIA discussed above and plays a pivotal role in investigating allegations pertaining to corruption, fraud and terrorism financing. One of the challenges experienced by the SLPF is the underreporting of corrupt criminal activity, resulting in few investigations and prosecutions.

Of interest to note is that St Lucia has not appeared on the Financial Action Task Force (FATF) list of countries that have been identified as having deficiencies in strategic anti money laundering (AML) initiatives. In May 2014, the country was recognised as having made significant progress in addressing and improving its AML and combating the finance of terrorism (CTFT) regime. This was evidenced by its legal and regulatory framework to meet its commitments as agreed in its Action Plan regarding strategic deficiencies previously identified by the Caribbean Financial Action Task Force (CFATF). As a result, St Lucia is no longer subject to rigorous CFATF or International Co-Operation Review Group (ICRG) monitoring.

6. Local and International Organisations

6.1 Civil society organisations

Civil society organisations (CSOs) play a vital role in the development of a country. Civil society is defined as the third sector, the government and private sector being the first and second sectors, respectively. However, this sector is not as developed in St Lucia as other larger Caribbean countries. This is a result of limited funding and the relative informality with which some organisations operate. Civil society activism and advocacy is more vibrant in some sectors, such as those involved in climate change, gender-based violence and lesbian, gay, bisexual, transsexual, questioning and intersex (LGBTQI) and HIV/AIDS issues. However, most of these organisations receive project funding from international donors such as the European Union, Commonwealth Foundation, United States Agency for International Development (USAID) and sector-based international donors, as well as state subventions.

Lack of core operational funding and limited staffing affect CSO's ability to engage in activities beyond the scope of grant-funded projects. It is noteworthy that St Lucia does not have an anti-corruption-specific type of CSO as in some of the larger Commonwealth Caribbean countries such as, for example, the Trinidad & Tobago Transparency Institute.

6.2 International organisations

Commonwealth Secretariat

In May 2018, St Lucia received Commonwealth Election Professionals (CEP) capacity-building for election officials through a programme focused on party financing, the independence of elections management body and encouraging wider participation of and involvement from women in running elections (Commonwealth Secretariat, 2021).

Caribbean Association of Integrity and Anti-Corruption Bodies (CCAICACB)

St Lucia is a member of CCAICACB, a regional organisation established with the aim to 'strengthen relations among the Commonwealth Caribbean countries in the areas of mutual legal assistance with the view that reciprocal exchange of expertise and information will enhance the prevention and combating of corruption in our respective countries' (Constitution CCAICACB, 2017).

United Nations

The United Nations Office on Drugs and Crime (UNODC), through the Centre of Excellence in Statistical Information on Government, Crime, Victimisation and Justice, conducted the Saint Lucia Crime Victimization Survey (SLNCVS,) which made St Lucia the first Caribbean country to measure victimisation in line with international United Nations standards. The data and wider learning from the survey emphasise the importance of implementing preventative measures against crime. (United Nations Office on Drugs & Crime, 2020).

In 2019, St Lucia presented its First Voluntary National Review Report (FVRR) on the Sustainable Development Goals (SDGs) at the United Nations High Political Forum. Under SDG 16 on peace, justice and strong institutions, reference is made to the fact that. '[the country] has made strides in implementing its promises through the national legal regime. There is an extremely low incidence of corruption in public office, with negligible allegations of administrative graft and prosecutions of public officers' (Government of St Lucia, 2019), p. 36).

7. Discussion

In continuing with its progress in building a robust anti-corruption regime, the Government should consider ways in which it is engaging with the various stakeholders to prevent corrupt practices occurring. These could include a clear policy mandate, systems to detect acts of corruption – i.e., financial disclosure systems for government and public officials – and public education programmes.

Policy mandate

The Government should have a clear policy mandate related to its fight against corruption. This helps all stakeholders to cooperate and work together. Among the persons interviewed, there were mixed perspectives as to whether anti-corruption was a policy mandate. One respondent stated that, 'Yes, I believe it's a priority', but went further to indicate that there were 'nearly no prosecutions'.

This view of no prosecutions was also shared by the respondent from law enforcement, who stated, 'I'm not sure how much of a priority this really is. The DPP will prosecute cases if they are brought forward – but they aren't.'

Prosecutions are linked to the reporting of corruption as well as the availability of data or statistics.

Financial disclosure system/ asset declarations

The Integrity in Public Life Act sets out the functions of the Integrity Commission, specifically in section 7, which says these include to receive, examine and retain all declarations filed. This system of asset declarations appears to be one of the key prevention measures to keep corruption of public officials at bay. It was raised by one media respondent, who stated that, 'Corruption has been addressed through the Declaration of Assets'.

At the same time, the respondent from law enforcement suggested that, 'the declaration of assets by those in public office is voluntary, and consequently many don't declare such'. However, while there may be a perception that the filing of declarations is voluntary, section 11(1) of the Act clearly states that,

> 'A person in public life shall, in accordance with this Act, file a declaration of income, assets and liabilities with the Commission in the manner prescribed in Form 2 of Schedule 3.'

Further reference to this mandatory requirement to declare can be found in section 13 and sanctions to be applied in section 20, which also includes the publication of the names of non-filers in the Gazette and local newspaper as well as referring the matter to the Director of Public Prosecutions for action.

One representative from the Integrity Commission indicated that in instances of initial non-filing, people whose names were published in the newspapers were embarrassed into action. As St Lucia is a small island where social connections are important, the publishing of names in the local newspapers creates a public or community exhortation to comply. Social interactions, in this case, leads to better compliance with the law and therefore, 'This gets people's attention' (Integrity Commission respondent).

As a further measure, the Integrity Commission seeks to assist declarants with the process and take a less legally sanctioned approach. This approach provides a better environment for enhancing compliance as the Commission works with declarants. As a result of this initiative, St Lucia saw an increase in forms being completed by MPs and senators for the period 2004 and 2015, as reported by the Chair of the Commission at the 5th CCAICACB Conference in 2019 (see Figure 4).

Public education

Another feature of a good anti-corruption programme is that of public education. This includes engagement with various stakeholders such as CSOs, schools and

Figure 4. Parliamentarians who filed declarations to the Integrity Commission, 2004–2015

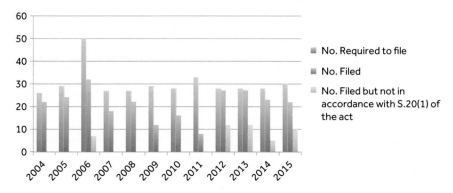

Source: St Lucia Country Paper, Caribbean Association of Integrity Commissions and Anti-Corruption Bodies Conference – 2019.

public agencies to enhance their knowledge about the work of the anti-corruption programme. Additionally, focus can range from awareness building to specific outreach on completing declaration forms and behavioural change activities to increase compliance, enhance overall citizen and public integrity and encourage the reporting of corruption.

The Integrity Commission also plans to devise a website, with a view to setting out its objectives and achievements and acting as a one-stop shop for citizens and others to access information.

The work of the Integrity Commission has focused recently on building integrity among the citizenry, as noted by the representative interviewed. Quite an effort was said to have been placed on public education campaigns and programmes in schools and across the Island over the years. An early success of this initiative was the production of the campaign handbook in 2005, entitled 'Unsatisfactory Completion of Declaration Forms', which was produced to provide guidance to persons in public life on how to complete the form satisfactorily (St Lucia Country Report – Commonwealth Caribbean Association of Integrity Commissions and Anti-Corruption Bodies Conference (2019).

Reporting

In order to provide appropriate sanctions, agencies such as the Integrity Commission depend on citizens to report acts of corruption. There were divergent views from the media representative and the respondent from law enforcement on this issue. Specifically, for the media representative,

> '…we have robust law enforcement and a crop of civil servants eager to report government level of corruption.'

Conversely, the representative from law enforcement noted that there was a lack of reporting on issues related to corruption. This view was supported by respondents from civil society and the Bar Association. Unfortunately, there were no statistical reports available to support or refute these statements.

Investigations

Conducting efficient and independent investigations into allegations of corruption plays a major role in creating public trust. Citizens require that law enforcement act independently to bring closure to reports. According to the media respondent, some investigations have been conducted. In one instance, this looked into the affairs of a politician with respect to the purchase of two properties. The case was investigated efficiently, and it was discovered that the politician had taken a loan for the purchase and did not illicitly acquire the funds.

It is also important when conducting investigations for agencies to cooperate and work closely on cases. The respondent from the Integrity Commission confirmed that the Commission collaborates with the police with respect to corruption allegations.

Enforcement and prosecutions

Connected to the theme of investigations is that of enforcement. Applying appropriate sanction for corrupt behaviours is of paramount importance to a successful anti-corruption regime. All respondents noted that lack of prosecutions,

> '…there is a low level of reports and no prosecutions. Accusations are consistently made by any sitting opposition.' (Media respondent)

This suggests that corruption allegations may sometimes be used as a means to scandalise politicians and have no real basis in fact. One respondent stated that in order to truly address the situation of corruption, political will is needed, but politicians only use corruption as an election weapon. When they are in power, they are in a position to change the system (but do not because they benefit).

The respondent from law enforcement compared enforcement and prosecutions to similar criminal acts in the private sector and actions taken,

> 'In the private sector, prosecutions have followed business owners reports of larceny by reason of employment, embezzlement and misuse of funds.'

Action taken by law enforcement with respect to reports from the private (rather than the public) sector is seen to be swift and effective. This may relate to the earlier point raised where corruption allegations are politically tainted and may not be factual.

Public procurement

Respondents noted although there had been an overhaul of the public procurement process recently, there were still issues in the government procurement process that have resulted in corruption allegations. One respondent commented on the recent St Jude Hospital reconstruction project: three years ago, financial and procedural discrepancies were observed in this incomplete project, which had cost EC$119 million. The cost should have been tendered but was done by direct award. The country subsequently became aware that there were deficiencies in the design and structural integrity of the building.

Citizen By Investment (CBI) Programme

St Lucia has a CBI programme through which investors can pay approximately US$200,000 to obtain citizenship within around 90 days following application (Transparency International and Global Witness, 2018). In recent years the CBI programme has been called into question as it is argued that such schemes provide safe havens for corrupt individuals fleeing prosecutions in their home countries (ibid.).

This has resulted in the country being criticised for not having rigorous vetting procedures in place and being placed on the OECD blacklist. In 2018, it was reported that a total of six individuals who were granted St Lucian citizenship through the CBI programme had their citizenship cancelled due to alleged involvement in acts that would harm the country's reputation (Pride, 2018).

8. Conclusion, Lessons, Challenges and Recommendations

There is no doubt that St Lucia has made positive strides to ensure that corruption is addressed. From the review of the institutional and legislative frameworks, it can be seen that it has enacted preventative measures such as asset declaration provisions and codes of ethical conduct to ensure that persons in public life are operating with integrity. Additionally, the Integrity Commission, the main anti-corruption agency, continues to roll out public education programmes toward building a culture of integrity.

With respect to criminalisation and sanctions, reporting of corruption appears to be very low. The reason for this is unclear. Additionally, the unavailability of statistical data on the effectiveness of enforcement measures affected the researcher's ability to clearly demonstrate impact. Nonetheless, the enforcement agencies and DPP remain ready and willing should there be reports of corruption submitted.

Overall, St Lucia has taken several positive legislative and institutional steps to curb corruption. These steps, along with those taken in AML and CFT, have been reflected in the consistently positive perception of anti-corruption efforts in the CPI over the years.

8.1 Lessons

Proactive and timely development of legislation

Based on the review conducted, it is clear that the Government has engaged in proactive reviews and the development of anti-corruption and associated laws. The most recent of these was the new procurement legislative, which sought to bridge several gaps in the former legislation.

Efforts by the Integrity Commission and other bodies through campaigning and lobbying the government to enact legislation have resulted in meaningful legislation coming on statute, including that regarding the declaration of assets.

Public education and awareness

The Integrity Commission has engaged in country-wide public education and awareness-building programmes focusing on the importance of 'integrity' and removing the emphasis purely on 'corruption'. This approach has a focus on everyone working and operating with integrity, which by extension places the burden on all citizens and stakeholders.

Independence of anti-corruption agencies

The anti-corruption agencies established in St Lucia – including the Integrity Commission, Office of the Director of Audit and the FIU – all operate independent of government. This ensures these agencies are able to function without government interference and further allows them to undertake their roles objectively.

Investigations

The anti-corruption legislation provides the remit for both the Integrity Commission and law enforcement agencies to undertake investigations related to allegations of corruption. This is crucial in building public trust and confidence that allegations of corruption will indeed be investigated. It is also important to highlight the importance of agencies working in partnership, as evidenced by the collaboration between the police and the Integrity Commission.

8.2 Limitations and challenges for this research

Limitations

Time: One of the main challenges to this research was the short timescale available to conduct the study, which was a short-term research consultancy. A more in-depth analysis would have required more time.

COVID-19 pandemic: The period of the study was also negatively affected by the COVID-19 pandemic. Travel to St Lucia and conducting face-to-face interviews were not possible. However, telephone and online interviews via Zoom were conducted as an alternative. The response rate was also affected as some respondents were unavailable to be interviewed due to other demands. In some instances, staff were working remotely and with limited core support.

Access to information: Connected to the prior point on the pandemic, documents and other pieces of information normally stored at offices could not be accessed to provide additional supporting evidence to the study. Consequently, there was a heavy reliance on open-source online research. Where possible, the respondent provided documentary evidence.

Challenges

In addition to the limitations listed above, there were some other challenges that affected the study.

Availability of key statistical data: By far one of the biggest challenges in this study was accessing statistical data on all of the key themes. The research depended almost entirely on data and documents available online through electronic platforms, and there was very little reporting of anti-corruption data available. None of the public agencies posted online data that could be used. Of note, there was no dedicated Integrity Commission website.

Low levels of reporting: In addition to the above, there were low levels of reports for acts of corruption. While there could be several reasons for this, it is important to note this fact.

No prosecutions: Together with the low levels of reporting, as stated above there were no prosecutions under the *Integrity in Public Life Act*.

8.3 Recommendations

Showcasing successes in the fight against corruption is important. St Lucia has shown significant progress over the past decade in this area through various initiatives. Arising from these efforts, the following recommendations should be considered across the wider Caribbean in tacking corruption:

- Open citizen public awareness anti-corruption seminars should be held annually across various parishes.

- All Caribbean countries should give due consideration to establishing a resourced Integrity Commission, if they have not already done so.

- Integrity Commissions should have a website that acts as a 'one stop shop' for the public and others to access information pertaining to anti-corruption.

- Outcomes of investigations should be published on the Integrity Commission website (as far as possible). This would go some way in building confidence and trust among citizens that issues of corruption are being taken seriously.

- A whistleblowing hotline should be introduced for persons to report anonymously.

- Consideration should be given to running anti-corruption reporting campaigns at key periods throughout the year.

The above mechanisms would assist the wider Caribbean in making further progress in addressing the ongoing challenges of corruption.

Bibliography

Akindele, ST (1995) 'Corruption: An Analytical Focus on the Problems of its Conceptualization'. *Ife Psychologia: An International Journal* 3(1): 55–69.

Alphonse, M (2018) 'Saint Lucia Airport Corruption Allegations Attract US Media Attention'. *St Lucia News*, 4 September.

Andersson, S and P Heywood (2009) 'The Politics of Perception. Use and Abuse of TI Approach to Measuring Corruption'. *Political Studies Association* 57(4): 746–767

Andrews, M (2008) 'Good Government Means Different Things in Different Countries'. Faculty Research Working Paper Series. Cambridge, MA: John. F. Kennedy School of Government, Harvard University.

Aveyard, H (2010) *Doing a Literature Review in Health and Social Care: A Practical Guide.* 2nd edition. Berkshire, UK: Open University Press.

Baxter, P and S Jack (2005) 'Qualitative Case Study Methodology: Study Design and Implementation for Novice Researchers'. *The Qualitative Report* 13(4): 544–559.

Berg, L (2007) *Qualitative Methods for the Social Sciences.* 6th edition. Long Beach, CA: California State University.

Commonwealth Secretariat (2021) 'St Lucia'. https://thecommonwealth.org/our-member-countries/saint-lucia

CSPL (Commission for Standards in Public Life) (2017) 'Constitution Guidelines'. http://www.standardsinpubliclifecommission.ky/constitutional-guidelines

Cresswell, J (2013) *Qualitative Inquiry & Research Design.* London; Sage.

Financial Intelligence Authority (2021) https://www.slufia.com/p/mission-vision -strategic-objectives

Freedom House (2021) 'St. Lucia'. https://freedomhouse.org/country/st-lucia

Government of St Lucia (2019) 'Saint Lucia: Voluntary National Review Report on the Implementation of the 2030 Agenda for Sustainable Development'. July. https://digitallibrary.un.org/record/3866737?ln=en

Hanson, H (2011) 'Managing Corruption Risks'. *Review of International Political Economy* 18(2): 251–275.

Heidenheimer, A (1978) *Political Corruption.* New Jersey: Transaction Publishers.

Johnston, M (1996) 'The Search for Definitions: The Vitality of Politics and the Issue of Corruption'. *International Science Journal* 149: 321–335.

Mauro, P (1995) 'Corruption and Growth'. *Quarterly Journal of Economics* 110(3): 681–712.

McCokser, H (2001) 'Undertaking Sensitive Research: Issues and Strategies for Meeting the Safety Needs of All Participants'. *Forum: Qualitative Social Research* 2(1): 2–7.

Miles, M and A Huberman (1994) Qualitative Data Analysis: An Expanded Sourcebook. 2nd edition. Thousand Oaks, CA: Sage Publication Inc.

Moody's Analytics (2021) 'St. Lucia'. https://www.economy.com/saint-lucia/investment

Monteduro, F, I Cecchetti, Y Lai and V Allergrini (2021) 'Does Stakeholder Engagement Affect Corruption Risk Management?' *Journal of Management and Governance* 25:759–785

Nye, S (1967) 'Corruption and Political Development: A Cost-Benefit Analysis'. *American Political Science Review* 61(2): 217-426.

Office of the Director of Audit (2021) https://auditstlucia.com/p/about-audit -saint-lucia

Pride (2018) 'St. Lucia Revokes Citizenship of Six People under Controversial CBI Programme'. 28 March. http://pridenews.ca/2018/03/28/st-lucia-revokes-citizenship-six-people-controversial-cbi-program/

St Lucia Country Report – 5th Annual Commonwealth Caribbean Association of Integrity Commissions and Anti-Corruption Bodies Conference (2019).

Transparency International and Global Witness (2018) *European Getaway: Inside the Murky World of Golden Visas.* Berlin: Transparency International. https://images. transparencycdn.org/images/2018_report_GoldenVisas_English.pdf

United Nations Office on Drugs and Crime (2020) 'UNODC Supports Saint Lucia in Generating Data on Victimization and Safety'. 3 July. https://www.unodc.org/ unodc/en/frontpage/2020/July/unodc-supports-saint-lucia-in-generating-data-on-victimization-and-safety.html

World Bank (2021) 'World Governance Indicators'. http://info.worldbank.org/ governance/wgi/

World Population Review (2021) 'St. Lucia'. https://worldpopulationreview.com/en/ countries/saint-lucia-population

Appendix: Interview Questions

Name:

Organisation:

Date/time:

Position in organisation:

1. St Lucia has been described to be one of the least corrupt countries in the Commonwealth. In your opinion, what do you think is responsible for this?

2. Corruption is typically defined as 'the abuse of entrusted power for private gain'. Therefore, combatting corruption in all its forms is important to (public institutions, civil society). How has your organisation played a role in combatting corruption in St Lucia?
    a. Public education

    b. Reform of the criminal justice system

    c. Law enforcement

    d. Prosecutions

    e. Providing funding

3. To what extent is anti-corruption a priority for the Government/Office of DPP/ Police/Integrity Commission/Financial Intelligence Unit of St Lucia?

4. How has your Government/Office of DPP/Police/Integrity Commission/ Financial Intelligence Unit addressed corruption in government and in the civil service?

5. What are some of the good practices that you and your Government/Office of DPP/Police/Integrity Commission/Financial Intelligence Unit have utilised to build public trust, transparency and accountability?

6. St Lucia is a signatory to both the International Convention against Corruption and United Nations Convention against Corruption. How has Government/ Office of DPP/Police/Integrity Commission/Financial Intelligence Unit engaged in international cooperation to combat corruption?

7. Do you believe that the present anti-corruption regime is sufficient to address the evolving nature of corruption domestically and internationally? Provide details.

8. If no, what are some of the proposals by the Government/Office of DPP/Police/ Integrity Commission/Financial Intelligence Unit?

9. Do you have any supporting documents you would like to share with us that may aid in our research?

10. Do you have anything further that you would like to share with us?

Chapter 7

St Vincent and the Grenadines

Matthew Goldie-Scott

Abstract

This report provides a broad overview of the context in which the research on combatting corruption has been undertaken in St Vincent and the Grenadines, with a brief summary of the methodology adopted, as well as the socio-economic and political context. There follows an examination of the legal context, noting positive achievements, while highlighting the potential for improvement in relation to the rule of law, as well as the perceived political neutrality of law enforcement. The institutional framework is also examined, noting widespread, bipartisan support for anti-corruption and integrity initiatives and highlighting the strong foundation this provides for future enhancements in these areas. The role of the private sector, media, civil society and other stakeholders is also examined, as well as those of international and regional organisations, and a range of tentative recommendations are set out that draw on the evidence reviewed.

1. Introduction

The component of the study on Combatting Corruption in the Commonwealth that focused on St Vincent and the Grenadines (SVG) began on 1 March 2021. This involved extensive review of relevant documents as well as consultations and interviews with key stakeholders to garner inputs and data. This report provides an overview of the findings arising from this research.

SVG is an island country located in the Caribbean, southeast of the Windward Islands of the Lesser Antilles in the West Indies, on the southern end of the Caribbean Sea where this converges with the Atlantic Ocean. It comprises the island of Saint Vincent and the northern Grenadines, 32 smaller islands and cays to the south (Commonwealth Secretariat, 2021). The population was estimated in 2018 to be around 110,211 (UN DESA, Population Division, 2019). The capital is Kingstown.

A member of the Commonwealth, SVG was historically a British colony and part of the West Indies Associated States from 1969 to 1979. It became an independent nation in 1979 and is a unitary parliamentary constitutional monarchy. The country is also a member of the Organization of American States (OAS), Organisation of Eastern Caribbean States (OECS) and Caribbean Community (CARICOM).

2. Methodology

This report has been prepared through a thorough process that sought to garner a wide range of pertinent evidence, to:

- Identify the impact made by key institutions in the fight against corruption:

- Discuss the extent to which key factors and institutions have been able to facilitate a whole-of-government approach to combatting corruption;

- Investigate how government institutions have worked with groups such as political parties, civil society organisations (CSOs), the media, development partners and the private sector in the course of their anti-corruption efforts; and

- Discuss how the lessons learned from this context could be applied elsewhere in the Commonwealth Caribbean.

This entailed:

- An in-depth review of existing literature pertaining to efforts to combat corruption in SVG;

- Extensive interviews with key stakeholders;

- Identification of the organisations and institutions that are driving anti-corruption; and

- Utilisation of a range of other appropriate research methodologies to gain access to the information required.

3. The Local Context

3.1 Corruption Perceptions Index

The Corruption Perceptions Index (CPI) score of SVG improved slightly between 2018 and 2019 (Table 1), though nonetheless declined overall since 2012 (Transparency International, 2021). It is one of the highest scoring countries in the region, ranking seventh, as well as being the fourth highest Commonwealth member state in the Caribbean and Americas, with only Canada, the Bahamas and Barbados achieving higher scores (ibid.). While there is scope for continued improvement, this represents a secure foundation on which to build future reforms and reflects a relatively high degree of perceived transparency, creating a positive environment in which anti-corruption initiatives can develop.

3.2 Political landscape

It is widely accepted that SVG is a functioning parliamentary democracy, i.e., it 'holds regular elections and has seen numerous transfers of power between parties', and

Table 1. SVG Corruption Perceptions Index score and rank, 2016–2020

Year	Corruption Perceptions Index score (out of 100)	Corruption Perceptions Index rank (global)
2020	59	40/180
2019	59	39/180
2018	58	41/180
2017	58	40/180
2016	60	35/176

Source: Transparency International, 2021.

'civil liberties are generally upheld' (Freedom House, 2020). The country has adopted a first-past-the-post electoral system and, as a result, the only parties to hold seats in Parliament are the Unity Labour Party (ULP) and the New Democratic Party (NDP). While no extra-political forces have been reported to interfere in elections, the Organization of American States (OAS) raised concerns in 2015 'about the lack of transparency regarding party and campaign financing, which could enable undue influence by private actors' (ibid.).

3.3 Economy

The country's economy is heavily dependent on agriculture and tourism, with the newly constructed Argyle International Airport opening in 2017 (Moody's Analytics, 2021). Much of the workforce is employed in banana production (which is potentially vulnerable, as a perishable good, to corrupt practices pertaining to facilitation payments), though this is likely to reduce significantly given the continued reduction of preferential access to markets in the European Union (IMF, 2004). This increases the likelihood of reliance on the small existing financial services industry (with associated compliance risks), as well as growing reliance on tourism (inevitably impacted significantly by restrictions implemented following the COVID-19 pandemic).

On 9 April 2021, the La Soufrière Volcano erupted, leading to approximately 16,000 individuals being evacuated (Associated Press and Wong, 2021). While resources have already been committed by the international community to provide assistance and support, the long-term economic impact of this event remains unclear (The New York Carib News, 2021). According to the Foreign, Commonwealth and Development Office (FCDO) (2021), as of October 2021 gross domestic product (GDP) per capita was US$7, 304.3 and real GDP growth was −3.3, with an annual inflation rate of −0.6 per cent.

3.4 Ease of doing business

According to the latest World Bank annual ratings, SVG is ranked 130 among 190 economies in ease of doing business (World Bank Group, 2020) (Table 2). The rank has remained unchanged since 2018, falling from 125 in 2016, while the score has improved from 56.9 in 2016 to 57.1 in 2020. The reporting on the ease of doing business also highlights a number of key strengths, with fairly high scores reported for 'starting a business', 'paying taxes' and 'trading across borders', as well as fairly strong outcomes for 'enforcing contracts' (ibid.). However, significant challenges were said to remain in relation to other activities, particularly 'dealing with construction permits', 'registering property' and 'getting credit', with particularly low outcomes in relation to 'resolving insolvency' (ibid.), although it is noted that there have been a range of legal mechanisms introduced to address deficiencies in this area (ibid.).

This has implications in relation to broader Commonwealth initiatives, particularly with regard to the scope for potential application of the newly published Commonwealth Anti-Corruption Benchmarks (Commonwealth Secretariat/ GIACC/ RICS, 2021), developed by the Commonwealth Secretariat in collaboration with the Global Infrastructure Anti-Corruption Centre (GIACC) and the Royal

Table 2. SVG Doing Business score and rank (2016–2020)

Year	Doing Business score	Doing Business rank
2020	57.1	130
2019	57.0	130
2018	56.9	130
2017	56.9	129
2016	56.9	125

Source: World Bank Group, 2020..

Institution of Chartered Surveyors (RICS), in consultation with the African Union, the International Monetary Fund (IMF), the United Nations Office on Drugs and Crime (UNODC) and Commonwealth law ministries, anti-corruption agencies and other partners. Released in April 2021, these set out good practice anti-corruption measures, specifically focused on infrastructure. As such, they serve as a tool for reviewing current practice and ensuring it is enhanced, where required, to ensure alignment with the Benchmarks. Given 'ease of doing business' challenges in pertinent areas, application of the benchmarks provides an excellent opportunity for positive reflection.

One stakeholder specifically noted the appropriateness of the Benchmarks to the context of SVG, stating:

> 'Well, they should implement the Benchmarks … It's all there: Requirement to have an independent A/C body, full transparency, political and public sector integrity measures, freedom of the press … Perhaps an audit by SVG against the Benchmarks [could be one of the report's key recommendations].'

3.5 Legal regime

The following key legislation has been identified as contributing to the fight against corruption:

The *Mutual Assistance in Criminal Matters Act, 1993* seeks to 'make provisions with respect to the scheme Relating to Mutual Assistance in Criminal Matters within the Commonwealth and to facilitate its operation in Saint Vincent and the Grenadines, and to make provision concerning mutual assistance in criminal matters between Saint Vincent and the Grenadines and countries other than Commonwealth countries'. The Act was signed between the Government and that of the United States and 'covers mutual legal assistance in criminal matters, as well as civil and administrative matters related to criminal proceedings' (Knowyourcountry.com, 2018).

The *Prevention of Corruption Act, 2004* is intended to prevent corruption 'in the performance of public functions and to give effect to the provisions of the Inter American Convention Against Corruption and to provide for matters incidental thereto or connected therewith'.

The *Finance Administration Act, 2004* seeks 'to provide for the management and control of public money, for the operation and control of the Consolidated Fund, for the establishment of a Contingencies Fund, for the authorisation of expenditures, for the establishment of special funds and deposit accounts, for the management and control of the public debt and the giving of guarantees, for the investment of public money, for the preparation of the Public Accounts, for the governance of statutory bodies, for the repeal of most of the provisions of the Finance and Audit Act, transitional matters and consequential amendments and to provide for matters connected therewith and incidental thereto'.

The *Financial Intelligence Unit Act, 2001* (amended in 2009) establishes a Financial Intelligence Unit (FIU) 'which will be the national centralised unit … for the collection, analysis and dissemination of suspicious transaction information to competent authorities'.

The *Proceeds of Crime Act, 2013* (amended in 2017) seeks to 'repeal and replace the *Proceeds of Crime and Money Laundering (Prevention) Act*, Chapter 173, with the intent of consolidating and updating the law relating to confiscation orders in relation to persons who benefit from criminal conduct, restraining orders to prohibit dealing with property, money laundering offences, Court orders to assist in investigations relating to money laundering or a person's benefit from criminal conduct and cooperation with overseas authorities and to introduce new provisions allowing for the recovery of property which is, or represents, property obtained through unlawful conduct and for incidental and connected purposes'.

The Anti-Money Laundering and Terrorist Financing Regulations, 2014 (amended in 2017) seek to 'provide for enhanced customer due diligence and ongoing monitoring for PE' (US Department of State Bureau of International Narcotics and Law Enforcement Affairs, 2019).

The *Anti-Terrorist Financing and Proliferation Act, 2015* (amended in 2017) seeks to 'repeal and replace the United Nations (Anti-Terrorism Measures) Act, Chapter 183, to update the law relating to the combatting of terrorist financing and for incidental and connected purposes'.

The Anti-Money Laundering Terrorist Financing Code, 2017 was designed 'to (a) criminalise money laundering; (b) provide for the confiscation of the proceeds of criminal conduct; (c) enable the civil recovery of property which represents, or is obtained through, unlawful conduct; (d) require persons in the financial sector to report knowledge or suspicions concerning money laundering to the FIU; (e) give the High Court the power to make a number of orders to assist the police in their investigations into money laundering; (f) continue the Confiscated Assets Fund; and (g) provide for the issuance of the Regulations and the Code to enable the establishment of a framework for the prevention and detection of money laundering and terrorist financing'.

The *Immigration (Restriction) (Amendment) Act, 2017* criminalises migrant smuggling (CFATF-GAFIC, 2018).

The *Public Procurement Act, 2018* is intended to 'provide for the general requirements in relation to public procurement, for exempt and partially exempt procurement, for the establishment of procurement authorities, for source selection, the solicitation procedures and the award of contracts, for the administration of contracts, for the assessment of procurement, for the review process; and to provide for connected and incidental matters' (House of Assembly, 2021a).

3.6 Institutional framework

The following key institutions have been identified as contributing to the fight against corruption.

The courts

The Eastern Caribbean Supreme Court (ECSC), established in 1967, 'administers the country's judicial system and assigns one High Court judges to reside in St Vincent and the Grenadines and hear cases from the country's courts' (DCAF, 2015). SVG is also a signatory to the Caribbean Court of Justice (CCJ), which was inaugurated in 2005 and serves as the judicial institution of the Caribbean Community (CARICOM) (ibid.). The Privy Council in London remains the country's court of final appeal (Freedom House, 2020).

Office of the Attorney General

The Office of the Attorney General was established more than two centuries ago. In 1979, the SVG's Constitution stipulated that 'the Attorney General is the principal legal adviser to the Government. He/she gives legal advice to the Prime Minister and his Cabinet who seek to govern the state lawfully and competently' (Ministry of Legal Affairs, 2021).

Office of the Director of Public Prosecutions

The Office of the Director of Public Prosecutions (ODPP) is the principal public prosecution service and its mission is '[t]o assist in the promotion of the highest standard of Criminal jurisprudence in Saint Vincent and the Grenadines and to effectively represent the Crown in all criminal procedures, whether by way of litigation or otherwise' (Government of Saint Vincent and the Grenadines, 2021). Established by the Constitution, it is headed by the Director of Public Prosecutions (DPP).

Audit Department

The Audit Department was established by the Constitution. Its objective is 'to examine the accounts of the Central Government, Local Government and Statutory Undertakings to ensure that funds provided by the Parliament are used for the purposes intended, giving due regard to economy, efficiency and effectiveness. It is intended that the Director of Audit reports on the accounts annually, which report forms the basis for the function of the Public Accounts Committee' (Audit Office, 2021).

Public Accounts Committee

A Public Accounts Committee is appointed by the House of Assembly at the commencement of each session. Its duties are to 'consider the accounts referred to section 75(2) of this Constitution in conjunction with the report of the Director of Audit and in particular to report to the House- (a) In the case of any excess or unauthorised expenditure of public funds the reasons for such expenditure, and (b) Any measures it considers necessary in order to ensure that public funds are properly spent, And such other duties relating to public accounts as the House may from time to time direct' (House of Assembly, 2021b).

Royal Saint Vincent and the Grenadines Police Force

The Royal Saint Vincent and the Grenadines Police Force dates back to 1834, when the *Police Act* provided for three divisions each with one sergeant and four men. Its mission is to 'ensure National Security by Preventing and Detecting Crime, Preserving the Public Peace and Protecting the Life and Property of the people of St Vincent and the Grenadines and its visitors, through effective Law Enforcement' (Royal Saint Vincent and the Grenadines Police Force, 2021).

Service Commissions Department

The Service Commissions Department is an autonomous government department that serves as the secretariat to the Public Service Commission. It consists of two divisions: the Personnel Division's responsibility is to 'support and enforce the rules and regulations of the Public Service as laid out in the Civil Service Orders', while the Training Division is responsible for 'allocating and providing training opportunities to the public' (Service Commissions Department, 2020).

SVG Human Rights Association (SVGHRA)

The SVG Human Rights Association (SVGHRA) 'is committed to promoting and protecting the civil, political, economic, social and cultural rights of the people of Saint Vincent and the Grenadines through education, training, representation, documentation and advocacy and by networking to influence the government and other agencies' (TakingITGlobal, 2015).

Regional and international organisations

The Organization of American States (OAS) was established in 1889 in order to achieve among its member states 'an order of peace and justice, to promote their solidarity, to strengthen their collaboration, and to defend their sovereignty, their territorial integrity, and their independence' (OAS, 2021b).

The Organisation of Eastern Caribbean States (OECS) is an inter-governmental organisation established in 1981 and dedicated to regional integration in the Eastern Caribbean. The vision of the organisation for 2020–2024 is 'A better quality of life for the people of the OECS' and its mission statement is 'To drive and support sustainable development through regional integration, collective action and development cooperation' (OECS, 2021).

The United Nations Convention Against Corruption (UNCAC) was adopted by the UN General Assembly in 2003 and came into force in 2005. It is the 'only legally binding universal anti-corruption instrument' and 'covers five main areas: preventive measures, criminalisation and law enforcement, international cooperation, asset recovery, and technical assistance and information exchange. The Convention covers many different forms of corruption, such as bribery, trading in influence, abuse of functions, and various acts of corruption in the private sector' (United Nations General Assembly, 2021).

The Caribbean Financial Action Task Force (CFATF) is a regional body established in 1996 that comprises 25 jurisdictions in the region that 'have agreed to implement the international standards for Anti-Money Laundering and Combating the Financing of Terrorism (AML/CFT)' (CFATF-GAFIC, 2018).

4. Analysis

4.1 Rule of law

In 2020, SVG ranked 31 out of 128 countries on the 'rule of law', rising four positions; 5 out of 30 countries in the Latin America and Caribbean region; and 2 out of 42 upper middle-income countries (World Justice Project, 2020).

In general, there is broad consensus that the judiciary generally operates independently. This broadly positive context notwithstanding, selected stakeholders continue to raise concerns over levels of transparency and the rule of law, with certain commentators in local media publications alleging 'mass corruption' and suggesting that 'a large proportion of voters are more than willing to accept bribes to vote in favour' of specific political parties (Green, 2020). Specifically, local media sources note allegations that votes were secured in exchange for 'twenty million dollars plus in building materials' (ibid.). While it should be noted that 'international observers from the Caribbean Community and the Organization of American States declared the elections generally free and fair' (U.S. Department of State Bureau of Democracy, Human Rights, and Labor, 2019; CARICOM, 2020), concerns were raised by the OAS in relation to the 'partiality of the presiding officer at the final vote count in the constituency of Central Leeward' in 2015, as well as 'a lack of transparency regarding party and campaign financing' (Freedom House, 2020).

Such concerns are reflected in a range of international appraisals of the local context, such as the U.S. Department of State 2019 Country Report, which suggests that while '[t]he law provides criminal penalties for corruption by officials… the government did not implement the law effectively', that '[o]fficials at times engaged in corrupt practices with impunity' and that there were '[a]llegations of political handouts', as well as alleged 'government corruption' and 'misappropriation of money allocated for aid and development program'. The report also notes that there 'are no financial disclosure laws for public officials' (U.S. Department of State Bureau of Democracy, Human Rights, and Labor, 2019).

This reflects a general belief that, while significant progress was made in 2009 in drafting integrity legislation (and garnering support for this from both incumbent and opposition politicians) – which included 'the establishment of a Commission to oversee the execution of the legislation' (Green, 2020), as well as a requirement that MPs 'declare their assets, liabilities, and income from every source to this Commission within three months of their election [and then] make a fresh submission by December 31 every year, while they serve in parliament' (ibid.) – an opportunity was potentially missed. Despite legislative drafting setting out a clear agenda to establish an Integrity Commission as early as 2004 (*Prevention of Corruption Act, 2004*), as well as commitments to participate in the Association of Integrity Commissions and Anti-Corruption Bodies in the Commonwealth Caribbean, with endorsement from the Commonwealth Secretariat in 2015 (Commonwealth Secretariat, 2015a), as of 2021, there is no Integrity Commission in place and the necessary legislation to facilitate its establishment has (while drafted) yet to be introduced. Likewise, Freedom of Information legislation, passed in 2003, has yet to be introduced, and it remains the case that 'there is no active legislation requiring government officials to disclose assets, income, or gifts' (Freedom House, 2020).

As such, the current 'oversight bodies' in SVG comprise 'the Office of the Attorney General, the Office of the Director of Public Prosecutions (DPP), the Director of Audit (DOA), and the Service Commissions Department of the Public Service Commissions (SCD)' (OAS, 2014a). A range of recommendations have been made for improvement in the effectiveness of these bodies, most notably in the 'Mechanism for Follow-Up on the Implementation of the Inter-American Convention Against Corruption' report (OAS, 2014b), which advocated a number of reforms, including:

'… establish inter-institutional coordination mechanisms to assist and ensure that public agencies abide by their legal obligation of requesting the Office of the Attorney General's legal advice in a timely and correct fashion, particularly in matters involving acts of corruption; work toward the drafting of legislative bills on transparency and anticorruption, dealing with, for instance, integrity in public service; and develop Office of the Attorney General-led policies and/or campaigns that would allow both public servants and the general population to develop a preventive attitude to ensure transparency and avoid acts of corruption.

'… provide the DOA with the human and financial resources necessary to ensure due compliance with its constitutional and legal duties, chiefly as regards conducting audits and detecting corrupt acts that trigger responsibility for the persons involved therein; take the steps necessary to ensure that those public agencies subject to the DOA's oversight effectively comply with the recommendations issued in its audit reports; strengthen control mechanisms of the DOA through the effective and timely implementation of the terms of section 22(1) of the Audit Act; and to adopt coordination and cooperation mechanisms to enable the DOA to send the DPP, the Royal Police Force, and/or the Financial Intelligence Unit, as applicable, timely notification of such evidence of corrupt acts that the DOA detects in the audits that it carries out.

'… take the steps necessary to conclude the effective implementation of the National Prosecution Service in order to strengthen, inter alia, the DPP's powers of supervision over procedures carried by police prosecutors; to implement coordination mechanisms between the DPP, the Royal Saint Vincent and the

Grenadines Police Force, the Office of the Attorney General, and the Financial Intelligence Unit, in order to establish effective and timely procedures and/or guidelines for exchanges of information and legal advice for the correct presentation before the courts of criminal proceedings related to acts of corruption; and to prepare statistical data on its duties and responsibilities.

'... consider updating the provisions that govern the [Service Commissions Department] SCD, in particular the Civil Service Orders for the Public Service of Saint Vincent and the Grenadines, which were enacted prior to the 1979 Constitution, and bringing them into line with the current standards necessary for the correct, honorable, and due performance of public functions; promote and regulate public reporting of acts of corruption in public service; and establish efficient and effective inter-institutional coordination to encourage and ensure that permanent secretaries, department heads, or other persons with the responsibility of doing so provide the SCD with the timely information it needs to perform its functions of disciplinary control and personnel administration within the public administration.' (OAS, 2014b)

4.2 Policing and law enforcement[1]

Broader concerns have also been noted, with the SVGHRA suggesting there is 'limited' corrupt activity and 'drug-related criminal activity among the police', but also that this is no longer 'a significant problem', with issues mainly pertaining to 'some officers ... tipping off drug dealers'. It expressed confidence that 'the police force will deal with errant members'. These sentiments have been echoed by other CSOs, with Marion House (a social services agency) expressing the view that, while 'police corruption and police involvement with drugs' remains 'an issue', 'once an officer is identified as being involved in corruption or drugs ... efforts are taken by government authorities to remove the officer from the force'. Nonetheless, external commentators, such as the U.S. Department of State, in the 2013 International Narcotics Control Strategy Report (INCSR), suggest this matter is not resolved, stating:

'No senior government officials in the Eastern Caribbean were prosecuted for engaging in or facilitating the illicit production or distribution of controlled drugs or laundering of proceeds from illegal drug transactions. Nonetheless, US analysts believe drug trafficking organizations elude law enforcement through bribery, influence, or coercion.'

However, it should be noted that, despite these concerns, this does not imply a culture in which such actions are undertaken with impunity, with the U.S. Department of State's Country Reports on Human Rights Practices for 2013 stating:

'Civilian authorities maintained effective control over the police, and the government has effective mechanisms to investigate and punish abuse and corruption. ... There were no verified reports of [police] impunity during the year, and the police chief suspended or dismissed officers from the police force for inappropriate conduct.'

The Commissioner of Police, commenting publicly on a case in which an officer was charged with dishonesty, expressed the hope that 'the general public will see that the hierarchy of the police force is doing all in their power to weed out the bad eggs and bring them to justice' (The Vincentian, 2014). Allegations against officers are addressed through 'an internal court system within the police force where a gazetted officer is assigned by the Commissioner of Police to hear the evidence against the defaulter who can be fined if found guilty', which appears to largely function effectively, though confidence in its independence could potentially be undermined by a structure that provides the Commissioner with the 'authority to amend' the decisions. Such concerns are particularly pronounced given that the role of Commissioner is effectively one that is politically appointed (GlobalSecurity.org, 2021).

Complains against the police are submitted by the public through the Public Relations and Complaints Department, or any police station, and are reported to be addressed effectively, though a lack of publicly available statistics on the number of prosecutions and convictions of police officers for misconduct or corruption has the potential to undermine the transparency of the process. The SVGHRA has called for a mechanism for monitoring police conduct that has greater transparency than the current system, and representatives of both the SVGHRA and Marion House state that there is no Ombudsman Office in place.

More broadly, a range of stakeholders, particularly police and human rights groups, have raised concerns over criminal perpetrators often making 'payoffs to victims of rape or sexual assault in exchange for victims not pressing charges' (U.S. Department of State Bureau of Democracy, Human Rights, and Labor, 2019) undermining confidence in the rule of law and access to justice for alleged victims.

4.3 Organisations, individuals and institutions driving anti-corruption initiatives

Civil society

As noted previously, the SVGHRA has been a vocal contributor to policy dialogue pertaining to corruption and transparency (Immigration and Refugee Board of Canada, 2014), and is reported by external stakeholders to have 'generally operated without government restriction, and investigated and published its findings on human rights cases' (U.S. Department of State Bureau of Democracy, Human Rights, and Labor, 2019, p. 6). In addition, the Government held 'various meetings with civil society that included the SVGHRA' (ibid.). Nonetheless, reports also suggest that such collaboration may be being undermined in some cases, with concerns raised that 'even where government officials shared the SVGHRA's concerns, [they] were intimidated by senior officials from investigating allegations of human rights abuses' (ibid.).

Likewise, organisations such as Marion House have contributed actively to policy dialogue and provided concrete recommendations on how transparency and anti-corruption initiatives could be strengthened (Immigration and Refugee Board of Canada, 2014). The National Council of Women has also made sustained and active contributions, particularly in relation to interactions with the OAS on anti-corruption matters (OAS, 2014b).

The media

Local and regional journalists have been proactive contributors to policy dialogue pertaining to corruption and transparency in SVG. While the state maintains ownership of the main local broadcaster, a range of private newspapers exist and there is widespread access to international news sources (Freedom House, 2020). Commentators note that '[t]he law provides for freedom of expression, including for the press, and the government generally respected this right. An independent press, an effective judiciary, and a functioning democratic political system combined to promote freedom of expression, including for the press' (U.S. Department of State Bureau of International Narcotics and Law Enforcement Affairs, 2019).

Concerns have been raised by some civil society representatives, however, that some parties may feel constrained in criticising the Government, 'primarily due to fear of facing libel charges, including under the 2016 Cybercrime Act. Civil society representatives indicated these fears resulted in media outlets practicing self-censorship. The Act establishes criminal penalties, including imprisonment, for offenses including libel by electronic communication, cyberbullying, and illegal acquisition of data' (ibid.). While it should be noted that '[t]he government did not charge anyone with libel or defamation', concerns exist throughout the Commonwealth over increased restrictions on freedom of speech (Free Speech Union, 2021), particularly with regard to restrictions on digital communication (especially when these entail significant legal sanctions); this is an area that warrants careful consideration. Press rights groups, including the International Press Institute have echoed these concerns, explicitly stating that:

> 'The St Vincent and the Grenadines House of Assembly should amend a pending cybercrime bill to provide stronger protection for freedom of expression and journalistic work in the public interest' (International Press Institute, 2016)

Specific concerns include 'vague language and the lack of a serious defence for journalistic work' (ibid.). Similar concerns over the *2016 Cybercrime Act* have been raised by Freedom House and reported by the BBC (2019).

Likewise, there have been concerns raised in relation to other avenues by which freedom of speech could potentially be undermined – specifically, in 2018, 'a magistrate granted a request by prosecutors to remand a woman to the Mental Health Rehabilitation Centre for psychiatric evaluation after she pleaded not guilty to a charge of abusive language. Her remarks had been directed at the wife of a senior government minister' (Freedom House, 2020).

While freedoms of peaceful assembly and association are protected in law, concerns were raised by some media and CSOs that 'citizens were hesitant to participate in anti-government protests due to fear of retaliation' (U.S. Department of State Bureau of Democracy, Human Rights, and Labor, 2019, p. 5). In such a context, it is essential that both perceived, and actual, freedom of press be prioritised to ensure that the media can continue to play a key role in facilitating transparency and constructive dialogue on policy reforms.

Development partners

Key donors to SVG have historically comprised the Caribbean Development Bank (CDB), the European Development Funding (EDF) programme, the Department for International Development (DFID), the International Bank for Reconstruction and Development (IBRD), the European Investment Bank (EIB) and the International Finance Corporation (IFC). Major bilateral assistance came from the Canadian International Development Agency (CIDA), USAID and the Government of Taiwan (Inter-American Development Bank, 2013). With DFID being incorporated into the newly formed Foreign, Commonwealth and Development Office (FCDO), the United Kingdom continues to serve as a major donor (FCDO, n.d.)

A range of stakeholders have suggested that there is scope for increased anti-corruption efforts under the auspices of the FCDO (Barrington, 2020), which would likely be of benefit to all partners, including SVG.

Likewise, the CDB has placed increasing emphasis on anti-corruption initiatives and has the capacity to serve as a clear partner in future reforms. In a welcome address to the Caribbean Conference on Corruption, Compliance and Cybercrime in 2020, the President said, inter alia, that,

> 'First, we want to engender increased understanding of the corrosive impact that corruption has on the economic and social development of emerging economies like those in our region. Second, we want to strengthen the response to corruption by enrolling institutions, individuals and groups which may not typically be at the forefront of anti-corruption initiatives but can play a critical role in the resolution. And third, we want to stimulate fresh ideas, new thinking, and innovative approaches to combatting this threat to our common future.

> 'To achieve these objectives, CDB must ensure that its loan and grant resources are used for the intended purposes and reach the intended beneficiaries. Unfortunately, this will not be sustainable if decision-makers, administrators, service providers and indeed the wider citizenry are not resolute in their commitment to uphold good governance in local, national, and regional institutions.

> 'Corruption matters, even when it is not in our peripheral vision. It matters to governments and corporate leaders because of the speed with which it can lead to significant financial and reputational damage and retard economic development. It matters to our youth, the next generation of employers, workers and service providers who will face constant temptation when they enter the workplace, and sometimes, even earlier. And it matters to our citizens who pay the price for corruption through reductions in the quantity and quality of social services, decaying infrastructure, and inefficient state institutions.' (Smith, 2020)

Similarly, USAID has emphasised the significance of continued anti-corruption, anti-money laundering and effective transparency provisions, as have a range of bilateral donors.

Private sector

The private sector has engaged proactively in dialogue relating to anti-corruption and transparency initiatives, including substantive consultations during the development of the SVG report on implementing the IACAC (OAS, 2014a). Noteworthy participants in such dialogue include (but are not limited to):

- The SVG Chamber of Industry and Commerce;

- The Bar Association of SVG; and

- The SVG Chamber of Agriculture & Nutrition. (OAS, 2014b)

Continued engagement with the private sector is essential if reforms are to be implemented effectively, particularly given the growing significance of the sector to national economic development (Ministry of Health, Wellness and the Environment, 2013).

Political parties

Positively, the two main political parties in SVG – the Unity Labour Party (ULP) and the New Democratic Party (NDP) – have consistently expressed bipartisan support for improved transparency and anti-corruption measures (Green, 2020), including broad endorsement of draft legislation to introduce an Integrity Commission, as well as mechanisms pertaining to declarations of assets, etc.

These initiatives have since stalled. As such, a clear opportunity exists to prioritise renewed efforts in this area as an apolitical, bipartisan approach to improving the transparency of the nation, thereby facilitating economic development and improved investor confidence.

Regional institutions

The OAS has played a key role in facilitating policy reform in the region and in SVG specifically (OAS, 2014b). There has also been continued regional collaboration with the Caribbean Financial Action Task Force (CFATF) on financial crime (CFATF-GAFIC, 2018). The latter noted in the CFATF XLVII May 2018 Plenary that it recognised that SVG has 'made significant progress in addressing the deficiencies identified in its 2010 Mutual Evaluation Report' and has therefore exited the follow-up process' (CFATF-GAFIC, 2018), encouraging the country 'to continue its progress towards strengthening its AML/CFT framework and ensuring that it is fully prepared for the 4th Round Mutual Evaluation' (ibid.). This is reflected by broader stakeholder assessments, noting that SVG 'continues to make progress with its AML regime [and] [t]he FIU has a good reputation in the Eastern Caribbean' (U.S. Department of State Bureau of International Narcotics and Law Enforcement Affairs, 2019).

Specifically, it has been highlighted that SVG has:

'comprehensive AML legislation and regulations, including the 2017 Proceeds of Crime (Amendment) Act and the 2017 Anti-Money Laundering Terrorist Financing Code. [It] has KYC [know your customer] and STR [suspicious transaction report] regulations. The 2014 Anti-Money Laundering and Terrorist Financing Regulations provide for enhanced customer due diligence and ongoing monitoring for PEPs [politically exposed persons]. In December 2017, the FIU revised its standard operating procedures regarding receipt, processing, and handling of sensitive information and requests. The main change requires financial analysts to process SARs [suspicious activity reports].' (Ibid.)

Stakeholders have also noted that work is already ongoing to 'address gaps in the 2017 Anti-Money Laundering and Terrorist Financing (Amendment) Regulations' (ibid.), and that consideration is also being given to measures to further regulate Designated Non-Financial Businesses and Professions (DNFBPs). The U.S. Department of State has suggested that SVG 'should become a party to the UNCAC', the United Nations Convention Against Corruption (ibid.).

Positive regional collaboration has been highlighted by a range of sources – specifically that, in 2018, 'FSA, FIU, and Eastern Caribbean Central Bank (ECCB) signed an MOU to facilitate collaboration, exchange of information, onsite examinations, and training' (ibid.)

Such initiatives also see continued support from bodies such as CARICOM (Commonwealth Secretariat, 2015b) and the Caribbean Development Bank (Caribbean Development Bank, 2020).

There are some avenues in which SVG has expressed a commitment to further collaboration but these have not yet been fully realised. They include initiatives that have been explicitly endorsed by the Commonwealth Secretariat, particularly participation in the Association of Integrity Commissions and Anti-Corruption Bodies in the Commonwealth Caribbean (Commonwealth Secretariat, 2015a), building on similar work elsewhere in the Commonwealth. In particular, this model draws on the approach taken in the formation of the Association of Anti-Corruption Agencies in Commonwealth Africa, which has 'helped improve the performance of national authorities through information exchanges, peer learning and by becoming a launch pad for bilateral agreements between countries' (ibid.).

In this context, active participation, following the establishment of a local Integrity Commission, in the Caribbean Association of Integrity Commissions would potentially be of significant benefit and facilitate the sharing of good practice and mutual lesson-learning and collaboration.

5. Key Lessons, Challenges and Recommendations

A set of key lessons, challenges and tentative recommendations arise in light of the current and historic context in SVG. These are addressed here in order of priority, with a view to maximising the likelihood of achieving 'quick wins' and facilitating lesson learning and collaboration throughout the region and the Commonwealth.

5.1 Lessons

Based on the above analysis of the legal, institutional and civil society context, SVG appears to have a satisfactory rule of law and widespread confidence in the capabilities of law enforcement agencies, which increases the likelihood of wrongdoers being reported and improves trust in the law. Additionally, the country has legislative frameworks that address anti money laundering, and it has been collaborating closely with the U.S. Department of State as well as other Commonwealth countries on anti-corruption initiatives and related criminal matters. These factors have contributed to a high outcome in terms of the CPI and Ease of Doing Business Index. The country continues to undertake reforms, and there appear to be good opportunities for bipartisan support for improved transparency and anti-corruption measures moving forward, thereby facilitating economic development, and improved investor confidence.

5.2 Challenges

Despite legislative drafting setting out a clear agenda to establish an Integrity Commission as early as 2004 (*Prevention of Corruption Act, 2004*), as well as commitments to participating in the Association of Integrity Commissions and Anti-Corruption Bodies in the Commonwealth Caribbean, with endorsement from the Commonwealth Secretariat in 2015 (Commonwealth Secretariat, 2015a), as of 2021, there is no Integrity Commission currently in place, and the necessary legislation to facilitate its establishment has (while drafted) yet to be introduced. Similarly, freedom of information legislation, passed in 2003, has yet to be introduced, and it remains the case that 'there is no active legislation requiring government officials to disclose assets, income, or gifts' (Freedom House, 2020).

Concerns have been raised over increased restrictions on freedom of speech (Free Speech Union, 2021), including reports of media outlets practicing self-censorship and feeling constrained in criticising the Government due to fear of facing libel charges under the *2016 Cybercrime Act*, which establishes criminal penalties for offenses including libel by electronic communication, cyberbullying and illegal acquisition of data. Citizens were also reported to be 'hesitant to participate in anti-government protests due to fear of retaliation' (U.S. Department of State Bureau of Democracy, Human Rights, and Labor, 2019).

Concerns have also been raised over the potential politicisation of the police force due to the introduction of a structure that provides authority to the politically appointed Commissioner of Police to amend a decision of the internal court system. This could potentially undermine confidence in the independence of the court system that allows allegations against police officers to be addressed.

While reporting on the ease of doing business in SVG highlights a number of key strengths, significant challenges remain in relation to activities such as 'dealing with construction permits', 'registering property' and 'getting credit', with particularly low outcomes in relation to 'resolving insolvency' (ibid.).

Finally, given declines in preferential access to European markets for agricultural exports, it is likely that the country's economy will become increasingly reliant on tourism, and that its financial services sector will grow. This brings economic opportunities, as well as challenges. It is important that both are anticipated in advance to ensure a legislative environment that promotes transparency and ease of doing business.

5.3 Recommendations

As one of the highest performing and least corrupt Commonwealth states in the region, SVG can serve as an example of good practice for its neighbours. As such, other countries looking to achieve similar outcomes should seek to replicate the examples of good practice highlighted in the preceding sections.

Given expressed bipartisan support for existing draft legislation from both major political parties, there is a clear opportunity for collaboration in enacting the draft integrity legislation and proceeding to form an Integrity Commission (as well as related commitments, such as enhanced disclosure requirements). This would allow for meaningful regional collaboration, through active participation in the Association of Integrity Commissions and Anti-Corruption Bodies in the Commonwealth Caribbean, as well as lesson-learning between this body and related entities elsewhere in the Commonwealth.

This also has the potential to address ongoing concerns from a wide range of stakeholders over a lack of effective legislative mechanisms to facilitate transparency and anti-corruption initiatives. In addition, it would facilitate a whole-of-government approach and serve as an example for the wider region as to the important role that integrity legislation, and associated commissions, can play in driving transparency efforts.

Freedom of the press must also be prioritised. There has been demonstrable engagement by journalists, and the press more broadly, in ongoing policy dialogue relating to transparency and corruption. Any factors undermining this have the potential to diminish confidence and detract from myriad successes. As such, it is essential that freedom of speech and of the press is protected and is seen to be protected. In particular, serious consideration should be given to recommendations from a wide range of stakeholders that the *2016 Cybercrime Act* should be amended to ensure clear protections for those seeking to hold leaders to account or to participate fully in meaningful debate.

The apolitical nature of law enforcement should be emphasised and enshrined in law. Concerns over the potential politicisation of the police force should be taken seriously, and steps should be taken to mitigate these concerns. Specifically, guidance should make it clear when political activity by public officials is acceptable (and, indeed, unacceptable), and the appointment process of the Commissioner should be rendered apolitical at the earliest opportunity.

The use of the newly published Commonwealth Anti-Corruption Benchmarks should be considered to ensure good practice in relation to infrastructure, particularly with regard to construction permits and registering property. Given concerns over ease of doing business in relation to these issues, it is recommended that the Benchmarks be utilised to undertake an in-depth review of legislative and procedural frameworks in these areas to ensure alignment with international good practice, increasing the likelihood of improvements.

Future shifts in the economic landscape should be considered carefully to ensure a robust framework is established to address future challenges. Continued collaboration, and consultation, with the private sector is essential if this process is to be successful.

Note

1   This section is based on Immigration and Board of Canada, 2014, and the sources cited can be found in that report.

Bibliography

Print and online publications

Associated Press and W Wong (2021) 'Explosive Eruption Rocks Volcano on Caribbean's St. Vincent'. NBC News, 9 April. https://www.nbcnews.com/news/world/st-vincent-evacuate-thousands-under-volcano-threat-n1263597

Audit Office (2021) 'Audit Office'. http://www.audit.gov.vc/audit/

Barrington, R (2020) 'How the New FCDO Could Advance the Fight against Corruption'. https://www.ids.ac.uk/opinions/how-the-new-fcdo-could-advance-the-fight-against-corruption/

BBC (2019) 'St Vincent and the Grenadines Profile: Media'. https://www.bbc.co.uk/news/world-latin-america-20006738

CARICOM (2020) 'CARICOM Election Observation Mission Declares the St. Vincent and the Grenadines Elections Free and Fair'. https://caricom.org/caricom-election-observation-mission-declares-the-st-vincent-and-the-grenadines-elections-free-and-fair/

CARICOM (2021) 'Member States and Associate Members'. https://caricom.org/member-states-and-associate-members/

CFATF (Caribbean Financial Access Task Force (2018) 'CFATF: Jurisdiction Exiting the Third Round of Mutual Evaluations'. https://www.cfatf-gafic.org/home-test/english-documents/cfatf-public-statements/9679-public-statement-and-notice-of-exiting-the-follow-up-process-may-2018/file

Commonwealth Secretariat (2015a) 'Caribbean Integrity Commissions Form New Commonwealth Body to Fight Corruption'. News, 25 June. https://thecommonwealth.org/media/news/caribbean-integrity-commissions-form-new-commonwealth-body-fight-corruption

Commonwealth Secretariat (2015b) 'Caribbean Anti-Corruption Commissions Gather at Commonwealth Conference'. News, 22 June https://thecommonwealth.

org/media/news/caribbean-anti-corruption-commissions-gather-commonwealth-conference

Commonwealth Secretariat, 2021. 'St Vincent and The Grenadines: Economy'. https://thecommonwealth.org/our-member-countries/st-vincent-and-grenadines/economy

Commonwealth Secretariat/GIACC (Global Infrastructure Anti-Corruption Centre)/RICS (Royal Institute for Chartered Surveyors) 2021 *Commonwealth Anti-Corruption Benchmarks*. London: Commonwealth Secretariat. https://giaccentre.org/chess_info/uploads/2021/04/COMMONWEALTH-BENCHMARKS.APRIL-2021.pdf

DCAF (Geneva Centre for Security Sector Governance) (2015) 'Saint Vincent and the Grenadines Country Profile'. https://issat.dcaf.ch/mkd/Learn/Resource-Library/Country-Profiles/Saint-Vincent-and-the-Grenadines-Country-Profile

FCDO (Foreign, Commonwealth and Development Office) (2021) 'St. Vincent and the Grenadines Economic Factsheet'. https://www.gov.uk/government/publications/st-vincent-and-the-grenadines-economic-factsheet

FCDO (Foreign, Commonwealth and Development Office) (n.d.) 'Development Tracker: St Vincent'. https://devtracker.fcdo.gov.uk/countries/VC

Free Speech Union (2021) 'Free Speech Union'. https://freespeechunion.org/

Freedom House (2020) *Freedom in the World 2020: St Vincent and the Grenadines*. https://freedomhouse.org/country/st-vincent-and-grenadines/freedom-world/2020

GlobalSecurity.org (2021) 'Saint Vincent – Corruption'. https://www.globalsecurity.org/military/world/caribbean/vc-corruption.htm

Government of Saint Vincent and the Grenadines (2021) 'Office of the DPP'. https://www.gov.vc/index.php/general-information

Green, N (2020) 'Mass Corruption in Saint Vincent'. *The New Today*, 20 June.

House of Assembly (2021a) 'Acts-2018'. http://assembly.gov.vc/assembly/images/Acts/Acts-2018.pdf

House of Assembly (2021b) 'Public Accounts Committee'. http://assembly.gov.vc/assembly/index.php/public-accounts-committee/48-public-accounts-committee-pac

Immigration and Refugee Board of Canada (2014) 'Saint Vincent and the Grenadines: Police Corruption and Misconduct, Including Involvement of Police Officers in Drug-related Criminal Activity; Procedures for Filing Complaints against Police Officers for Corruption, Inaction or Misconduct (2011–October 2014)'. https://www.refworld.org/docid/548167a44.html

IMF (International Monetary Fund) (2004) 'Eastern Caribbean Currency Union: Selected Issues'. 27 October. https://www.imf.org/en/Publications/CR/Issues/2016/12/31/Eastern-Caribbean-Currency-Union-Selected-Issues-17805

Inter-American Development Bank (2013) 'Donor Matrix: St. Vincent and the Grenadines'. https://www.competecaribbean.org/documents/donor-matrix-saint-vincent-and-the-grenadines-2013/

International Press Institute (2016) 'St. Vincent and Grenadines Urged to Amend Cybercrime Bill'. https://ipi.media/st-vincent-and-grenadines-urged-to-amend- cybercrime-bill/

Knowyourcountry.com (2018) 'St Vincent & the Grenadines Risk & Compliance'. Report.

Ministry of Health, Wellness and the Environment (2013) *National Report St. Vincent and the Grenadines: Third International Conference on Small Island Developing States.* July. https://wedocs.unep.org/bitstream/handle/20.500.11822/8530/StVincentand TheGrenadines.pdf?sequence=3&isAllowed=y

Ministry of Legal Affairs (2021) 'About Us'. http://legal.gov.vc/legal/index.php/history

Moody's Analytics (2021) 'Saint Vincent and the Grenadines: Economic Indicators'. https://www.economy.com/saint-vincent-and-the-grenadines/indicators#ECONOMY

OAS (Organization of American States) (2014a) 'OAS Anti-Corruption Mechanism Released Report on Saint Vincent and the Grenadines'. Press Release, 17 September. https://www.oas.org/en/media_center/press_release.asp?sCodigo=E-377/14

OAS (Organization of American States) (2014b) *Report on Implementation in Saint Vincent and the Grenadines of the Convention Provision Selected for Review in the Fourth Round, and on Follow-Up to the Recommendations Formulated to that Country in the First Round.* http://www.oas.org/juridico/PDFs/mesicic4_final_svg_en.pdf

OAS (Organization of American States) (2021) 'About the OAS'. http://www.oas.org/en/about/who_we_are.asp

OAS (Organization of American States) and CICAD (Inter-American Drug Abuse Control Mechanism (2019) *Saint Vincent and the Grenadines: Evaluation Report on Drug Policies 2019.* Washington, DC: OAS and CICAD. http://www.cicad.oas.org/mem/reports/7/Full_Eval/St_Vincent_and_the_Grenadines-7thRd-ENG.pdf

OECS (Organisation of Eastern Caribbean States) (2021) 'About the OECS'. https://oecs.org/en/who-we-are/about-us

Royal Saint Vincent and the Grenadines Police Force (2021) 'About Us'. http://rsvgpf.gov.vc/rsvgpf/index.php/mission-and-vision-statement

Service Commissions Department (2020). 'Home'. http://www.psc.gov.vc/psc/

Smith, WW (2020) 'Welcome: Caribbean Conference on Corruption, Compliance, and Cybercrime' Speech by the President, Caribbean Development Bank. https://www.caribank.org/newsroom/news-and-events/speeches/welcome-caribbean-conference-corruption-compliance- and-cybercrime

TakingITGlobal (2015) 'SVG-Human Rights Association'. https://orgs.tigweb.org/svghuman-rights-association

The New York Carib News (2021) 'US$20m for St. Vincent Volcano Response from World Bank'. 13 April. https://www.nycaribnews.com/articles/us20m-for-st-vincent-volcano-response-from-world-bank/

Transparency International (2021) 'Corruption Perceptions Index'. https://www.transparency.org/en/cpi/2020/index/vct

UN DESA (Department of Economic and Social Affairs), Population Division (2019) *World Population Prospects 2019.* https://population.un.org/wpp/

United Nations General Assembly (2021) *United Nations Convention against Corruption.* https://www.unodc.org/unodc/en/corruption/uncac.html

U.S. Department of State Bureau of Democracy, Human Rights, and Labor (2019) 2019 *Country Reports on Human Rights Practices: Saint Vincent and the Grenadinesv.* https://www.state.gov/reports/2019-country-reports-on-human-rights-practices/saint-vincent-and-the-grenadines/

U.S. Department of State Bureau of International Narcotics and Law Enforcement Affairs (2019) *International Narcotics Control Strategy Report: Volume II – Money Laundering.* https://www.state.gov/wp-content/uploads/2019/03/INCSR-Vol-INCSR-Vol.-2-pdf.pdf

World Bank Group (2020) *Doing Business 2020: Economy Profile – St. Vincent and the Grenadines.* Washington, DC: World Bank. https://www.doingbusiness.org/content/dam/doingBusiness/country/s/st-vincent-and-the-grenadines/VCT.pdf

World Justice Project (2020) 'St. Vincent and the Grenadines Ranked 31 out of 128 Countries on Rule of Law, Rising Four Positions'. 11 March. https://worldjusticeproject.org/sites/default/files/documents/St.%20Vincent%20and%20the%20Grenadines%20-%202020%20WJP%20Rule%20of%20Law%20Index%20Country%20Press%20Release.pdf

Legislation

Anti-Money Laundering Terrorist Financing Code, 2017

Anti-Terrorist Financing and Proliferation Act, 2015

Finance Administration Act, 2004

Financial Intelligence Unit Act, 2009

Prevention of Corruption Act, 2004

Proceeds of Crime Act, 2013

The Mutual Assistance in Criminal Matters Act, 1993